OVERVIEW OF DISCIPLESHIP IN DISCIPLING MUSLIM BACKGROUND BELIEVERS

Abu Da'ud

Overview of Discipleship in Discipling Muslim Background Believers

ISBN: 978-1-950254-09-5
eISBN: 978-1-950254-10-1
eISBN: 978-1-950254-11-8

All Bible quotations are from the World English Bible, which is not copyrighted. It is in the public domain for both print and electronic formats.

Table of Contents

INTRODUCTION

This book accompanies the Muslim ministry handbook *Discipling Muslim Background Believers*. It describes discipling Muslim background believers ("MBBs"), evangelizing Muslims, starting small groups and churches, as well as dealing with persecution and being a secret believer for a period. Though this book may deal with those topics to an extent, it is just an overview.

Discipling Muslim Background Believers is in an easily referenced handbook format, while this book will describe discipling MBBs in prose. This book will give the reader a good overview of discipling MBBs, but will not provide the MBB with the ability to answer critical questions independently – which *Discipling Muslim Background Believers* does. I highly recommend using this book as a means of getting a broad overview of discipling MBBs, and using both *Discipling Muslim Background Believers* and my accompanying Bible study –*Muslim Background Believer Discipleship Bible Studies* –with the MBB. The Bible studies will help the MBB reflect on important Bible verses regarding important growth areas and will also specifically refer to sections in the handbook for further reference.

If you are unfamiliar with Islamic beliefs, please research the six articles of belief and the five pillars of Islam by clicking on the appropriate link on the blog page of my website, abudaud.com.

This book does not contain legal, psychological or medical advice. None of the suggestions are intended as guarantees that you will experience any type of intended result.

Bold text is used in body paragraphs in this book to indicate concepts or phrases dealt with more fully in *Discipling Muslim Background Believers*.

1 SOME CONSIDERATIONS FOR THE DISCIPLER

Please read through this book and be familiar with its concepts before ministering to an MBB. As you read it, if you feel that you would like more explanation, please refer to my book *Discipling Muslim Background Believers*.

There is no required timetable for the lessons in this book. Please disciple the MBB at the rate that best fits the circumstances.

You can best serve the MBB by determining their level of independent thinking and the level of opposition to converts that might be in the MBB's community. The diagnostic questions below can help you do so.

1.1 DIAGNOSTIC QUESTIONS

You can frame questions to determine the MBB's level of independent thinking and the likely strength of their community's opposition by asking things like:

- Was your view of God before coming to Christ based mainly on what you have heard from others or your own thinking/study/research? On a scale of 1-

10 (10 being completely based on your efforts), how much is based on your own thinking/study/research?

- Does your family (tribe, culture, country, town or village) feel the same way about God?
  You can also ask the same question about parents, brothers, sisters, etc.
- How would/do they react if someone left the family (tribe, culture, country, town or village) religion?

The answers to the above can help the MBB better understand the MBB's mindset and their likelihood and extent of persecution. They can also be used to identify **similarly situated MBBs**.

If you or the MBB feel that the MBB may be persecuted, the MBB will be well served by becoming a **secret believer** for a while – meaning they keep their faith confidential while living a Bible-based life. Please refer to my book *Discipling Muslim Background Believers*. It is very important to do so because the book contains details on how to be a secret believer, the extensive preparation and planning needed, as well as what to do if things go badly wrong.

If you think it is possible that the MBB may need to separate from you because of persecution or may be isolated from outsiders, then please ensure that they at least have a copy of my book *Discipling Muslim Background Believers*. It contains easily-referenced sections in a handbook format that are useful for quickly answering questions. It also contains a table containing a list of sections that they can read that will provide them scripture and explanation for practically living a Christian life. There is also material in that book that will teach them evangelism methods, how to start and grow small groups, and even to start churches. If you are separated from the MBB, the book explains ways that you and the MBB can use to communicate confidentially. You can then refer to specific sections and discuss them as you are able.

Some of the first things to teach a new MBB or one that knows little of the Christian faith are basic truths about Christianity. Given the extensive misunderstanding many Muslims have about Christianity, it is very important to correct their misconceptions about their new faith. Chapter 3 of this book covers some of those areas.

2   SOME CONSIDERATIONS FOR THE DISCIPLE

Please read through the Table of Contents so that you know what topics will be covered. If you want to learn a particular topic out of the suggested order, you will be able to find it.

If someone is discipling you, it is best to read the material prior to discussing it with them. Doing so will make your meetings more productive than if you have not properly prepared.

3 UNDERSTANDING SOME OF THE BASICS OF CHRISTIANITY

God is good, and created mankind in order to love and bless them. **His purpose** was loving because **He is love**. God is **all powerful** and **just**. He requires payment for **sin** – disobeying Him – even though He is **merciful**. God is **one God**. He has **one essence and three persons** that each have all of God's attributes. He is **Father**, **Son** and **Holy Spirit**. The Son is **Jesus Christ** the Messiah.

God created **Adam** and **Eve**. Adam sinned by eating fruit from the tree of the knowledge of good and evil. Through Adam's sin, **all of mankind sinned because we were all in Adam**. Not only did mankind fall, but we now live in a **fallen world** because of his sin. God wanted good things for us but knew that they would not come to us because mankind's nature had become evil when Adam sinned. We could and would choose wrongly by **nature**. God knew that mankind's sins needed to be paid for and man's natural drive to disobey needed to be removed in order for mankind to enjoy the benefits that He wanted to give to them. He already had the plan in place to fix the problems that mankind created. In His **mercy** and foreknowledge, God paid our penalty by giving the life of His son, Jesus Christ before the foundation of the world.

It is important to note that before time began, God knew each one of us, and the life sacrificed – Jesus' – paid for each one of us individually by dying and then rising again three days later to give us life.

God is the God of **Abraham**, **Isaac** and **Jacob**. He made a **covenant** with Abraham when he was willing to **sacrifice his son, Isaac** (not Ishmael). God is a God who keeps His word and His covenants.

God gave another covenant to **Moses**. That covenant required that people follow the regulations and rules of the Law, including the **Ten Commandments**. The Law contained penalties for sin, meaning that the Law created **guilt** – a penalty – for sin, and people began to feel **shame** – a negative feeling regarding their own worth because they had done something against God. Even breaking one small part of the Law meant that they were **guilty of breaking all of it**. That meant that every sin carried with it the **penalty of physical death** and also **eternal separation from God** because they were law-breakers. God's perfection would not tolerate law-breakers to be present with Him for eternity. One of God's purposes in this covenant was to lead people to Himself by showing mankind that they needed a savior because they could not be perfect. There were other covenants, but the most important one came in Jesus Christ the Messiah. That is called the new covenant, with the old one being embodied in the Law. The old covenant is also referred to as the **Old Testament**, and the new covenant is also referred to as the **New Testament**.

Jesus Christ the Messiah **became a man**. He was **born** of **Mary**, and God created Him within her womb. There was no sexual activity. He was the **fulness of God** in bodily form. He was man and God at the same time, and was indwelt by and anointed by the Holy Spirit. Jesus Christ the Messiah lived a sinless life. He was **crucified** to pay for our sins, and was **resurrected** by the Holy Spirit to give us life. He then ascended to heaven. A person can experience **forgiveness** of sin, have their **nature changed** and receive the life that God has for us by believing **essential Christian beliefs** (*see below* in chapter on sharing your faith); **confessing** their sin; **repenting** of it and any other religion; turning to God; confessing Jesus Christ as **Lord**; and following Him by obeying His commands and His ways. His commands and ways can be learned by reading and understanding the Bible (*see below*).

A person who follows Jesus Christ the Messiah as Lord and Savior has **salvation**, a **new nature** that is **righteous** – it has a good standing with God, meaning that He welcomes the righteous into His presence. This person is a Christian. Christians still sin, but it is by choice rather than by nature. If a Christian sins, he or she can **repent** and be forgiven. Forgiveness means that the payment of Jesus' blood on the cross removes your guilt and shame, making things right with

God as if you had never sinned. Forgiveness is part of God's **mercy**, which is His undeserved **favor** – God's desire to be good to an individual.

Christians live the life that God has called them to by **faith** – being fully persuaded about God. They are **filled** with God's Holy Spirit, who also **anoints** them for service. God gives Christians the desire and the ability to do the things He asks. That desire and ability is known as **grace**.

It is important for a Christian to know how to **pray** – ask God for things – and **hear from God** so that he or she can **fellowship with God**, learn and **be led by Him**, and ask for things. Please generally follow the order of this book, but you may find it useful to read the lessons on intimacy with God, hearing God and prayer out of order.

4 READING AND UNDERSTANDING THE BIBLE

The **Bible** is the inerrant word of God. It can be read and understood by any person who can read. The Holy Spirit will guide the reader who is open to His leading. One of the first things to know is that the Bible is accurate.

4.1 THE BIBLE YOU HAVE IS ACCURATE

The argument regarding accuracy is important in knowing whether the Bible is in its true form. Rather than reproduce the argument, I will refer you to Josh McDowell's book, *New Evidence That Demands a Verdict*, which devotes over 100 pages to making a case for the Bible. There are many other books that make a similar case.

To understand the Bible, it is useful to know its structure.

4.2 THE STRUCTURE OF THE BIBLE

The Bible is made up of sixty-six books by more than forty authors whose source was inspiration from God.

It was written between approximately 1,500 B.C. to 100 A.D., a total of about 1,600 years. However, there was a period of about 400 years prior to the birth of Christ during which no books were written.

Of the sixty-six books, thirty-nine are in the Old Testament and twenty-seven are in the New Testament.

In the Old Testament, the thirty-nine books are categorized as follows:

- The Law – Genesis to Deuteronomy (five books). The Abrahamic covenant, the giving of the Law – to Moses, and Israel's obedience and disobedience of the Law.

- Histories – Joshua to Esther (twelve books). The history of the tribes of Israel after entering the promised land and the dividing of Israel into two kingdoms and Israel's exile.

- Wisdom Literature – Job to Song of Solomon (five books). Contain general wisdom often in the form of poetry. The Psalms are filled with laments, prayers, praise and thanksgiving and reveal how God acted in various circumstances. The Proverbs are an excellent resource for getting general and specific direction in various circumstances.

- Prophets – Isaiah to Malachi (seventeen books). Contain prophecies, including about Israel's restoration, the new covenant, the Son of God, and the end times.

In the New Testament, the twenty-seven books are categorized as follows:

- Gospels – Matthew to John (four books). Describe the birth, life, ministry, death and resurrection of Jesus Christ the Messiah and contain His teachings.
- Acts – Acts (one book). While called the Acts of the Apostles, also describes the work of the Holy Spirit through the apostles and the early growth of the church.
- Letters (epistles) – Romans to Jude (twenty-one books). Letters to churches, Christians working to grow the church, and general letters. They all contain doctrine and practice, and help the reader understand and follow Jesus' teachings.
- Revelation – Revelation (one book). The revelation concerning the end times given to the apostle John while on the island of Patmos.

If you see a Bible reference, it will be in a Book chapter:verse format, and may be abbreviated. Thus, Jer. 29:11 WEB refers to the book of Jeremiah, the 29th chapter and the 11th verse in the World English Bible version of the Bible.

4.3   HOW DO I READ, INTERPRET AND APPLY THE BIBLE?

Please note that reading things in the Bible once is not enough because God will often show new things each time you read it.

4.3.1   DEVOTIONAL READING

It is useful to both study the Bible and read devotionally. Devotional reading is reading simply to relate to the Lord and find out more about Him. It is usually not very in-depth, even though deep thoughts can occur during it. It is unlikely that you will use Bible study aids during devotional reading time.

If you are new to the Bible, or relatively new to it, please consider reading about God Jesus, the Holy Spirit, the Trinity and some of the **key people** in the Bible. Then please consider reading the Bible for the first time through much the way you would a novel. This first reading will let you put Bible stories into context, as well as the teachings of the Bible. I would recommend then reading it through quickly two more times, with slightly different purposes. The second time is to understand the teachings and stories, and to break them down into manageable pieces. The third time is to put all the pieces into a good framework in your mind. With this background, Bible reading and study is more effective.

If you are familiar with the Bible, read chapters from the Old Testament and the New Testament, as well as some of the wisdom literature. The latter will help in making decisions, while reading the Old and New Testaments will help understand the teachings and history as well as the main characters of the Bible.

I also recommend reading one chapter of the Old Testament (starting with the first chapter of Genesis), one chapter of the New Testament (starting with John - not Matthew because then you will read four books that contain very similar stories), five chapters in Psalms (these are usually quite short, more like poems) and one chapter of Proverbs. As you can see, you'll read Psalms and Proverbs completely almost every month.

If you can, in addition to your devotional reading, you should spend some time studying the Bible.

4.3.2 SOME SUGGESTIONS FOR STUDYING THE BIBLE

One of the key things to do when studying or reading the Bible is to look for the purpose behind what was written. The overall purpose of the Bible is so that the reader can know God. This is true both for the seeker and for the Christian. That purpose should be kept in mind regardless of what part of the Bible you are reading.

Each book also has a purpose. It is instructive to try to find it. Bible study aids are very useful in providing this type of information. They can be found online, and I also mention a few of them below.

Look for overarching messages in books, histories and stories. Also look for themes and repeated themes.

Note that Bible prophecies can be fulfilled during the time they were spoken, can also have a future fulfillment in Jesus, or His church (the Christian population at large is referred to as His church, and local congregations can be called churches – here I am referring to the large population).

Be very disciplined in interpreting analogy and metaphor in the Bible. The interpretation must be consistent with the whole of the Bible.

In the New Testament letters, there are often arguments being made by the writers that span more than one chapter. Please be aware that the books of the Bible did not contain the reference system. That was put in later by scribes so that it would be easier to refer to specific parts and verses of the Bible. The reason to mention that in this context is that an argument does not necessarily end when the chapter in the Bible ends. For instance, Paul makes a long argument in Romans 3-7, with chapter 7 referring to himself prior to conversion. Then in chapter 8 he begins to talk about what a Christian looks like in contrast to someone prior to conversion – what he had described in chapter 7. Though the subject changes, it is important to see the argument spans the chapter break.

Each word in the Bible is important in building up the verses, chapters, and books. Sometimes it is useful to look up every word in a sentence or even a paragraph to understand what the writer is saying. Words can be looked up in a Bible dictionary or even in an interlinear Bible. An interlinear Bible will show the original language and a word-for-word translation in your language. It is even better to use an interlinear Bible online, because you can then click on the original language and find out exactly what that word means, and if you have difficulty there are usually links to special commentaries.

Once you understand a sentence, link it to other sentences, noting how your understanding changes. Repeat the process for paragraphs, sections and then entire books. After you have read the Bible, you will see patterns that repeat, stories and concepts that link across books of the Bible, and throughout you will see God's love for mankind, and His story of redemption and victory for all mankind. While not all people will take what is offered, His offer is clear in the Bible.

Once you have read, studied and understood a passage, please keep coming back to read it and study it periodically. Your interpretation and understanding of it will change as you understand more of the rest of the Bible, as you grow as a Christian, as your circumstances and perception change, and as God inspires you differently than before while you read and study. I am not saying that the word of God will change. The Holy Spirit is often surgical in the way He allows you to see, experience and understand the Bible. He may highlight very specific parts of it depending on your circumstances. God's word does not change depending on our circumstances. Our understanding of it might.

There are many different ways to study the Bible. One way is to focus on a specific person in the Bible. Another way is to focus on a particular story, such as what happened when David killed Goliath. Another way to study is to focus on a specific word in a verse or the use of that word throughout the Bible. You can also focus on themes, a book or books of the Bible, or specific passages of the Bible.

4.3.3   BIBLE STUDY AIDS

There are many types of Bible study aid. Most are available online. I find that I mostly use commentaries (which contain expert analysis and interpretation of the Bible), Bible dictionaries (which contain definitions of Bible words), or search capabilities that help me find Bible information. I find my Bible app and free search engines such as Google to be very helpful in locating specific Bible verses using search terms.

Please also use an interlinear (one with the original text over or under the translated language) Bible, a Bible dictionary and a lexicon (these show how the word is used) to verify the translation that you are reading. You can find these online for free and also in various apps.

YouVersion is the free Bible app that I use. *BibleGateway* is an excellent online resource with a good selection of Bible study aids. *BibleHub*, another online resource, has excellent interlinear material.

4.3.4   MEMORIZATION

When memorizing, focus on remembering the meaning of the verses as well as the words. Memorizing verses or portions of the Bible (*see* **12.12 MEMORIZING BIBLE VERSES**) can be helpful when meditating on the verse or verses to try to understand them. Memorization can also be helpful when discussing with others. Please remember the reference so that you can locate it again and also tell others where the verse is.

Writing the scripture on paper or cards is useful so that you can carry the verse(s) with you and refer to them often as you try to memorize them. If you have a smart phone, a Bible app is helpful for reading and memorization. There are many that are free, including the one I use, *YouVersion*. It contains many translations of the Bible in many languages.

Songs, poems, and stories are often easier to remember than words of prose on a page. You can make up your own songs or poems to memorize the words from the Bible, or use ones that are already well-established.

4.3.5   MEDITATING ON THE BIBLE

Meditating on the Bible means to intentionally think through words, phrases, passages, stories themes and other aspects of the Bible by continuing to ponder and think for long periods about those aspects. This type of thinking gets stronger with time, and can help understand the Bible better.

This type of thinking is not like chewing a bite of food in which the person's goal is to spend just a little time and get it swallowed. Rather, this type of thinking is like chewing something for flavor, and keeping it in one's mouth. Each time it is chewed, the food yields a little more flavor. The word of God is like a flavorful bite that keeps yielding flavor as we intentionally chew on it.

Our chewing/pondering must be active – not simply repeating the words in our head and expecting meaning to flow. The person seeking meaning must actively break down the words and passages. If no more meaning is forthcoming, then use Bible study aids. Once the meaning is gained, ponder the meaning, and seek to apply it to your life. Proper application and spiritual growth are the end goal of meditation.

It is important to apply the Bible to our lives, **conforming our thoughts to the teaching of the Bible**, and **living according to the values in it**.

Part of doing the above paragraph is learning **God's promises** and **how He applies them to our lives**.

5 GOD IS A KEEPER OF COVENANTS

God is **faithful** – it is part of His nature. He keeps **covenants** as a result of His nature. Some of the covenants, like the Law, are **bilateral** – there are responsibilities on both sides. The Lord said if we keep the Law, then He blesses us. If we perform our responsibility, He performs His promise. If we break our promise, He punishes us. That is the Old Covenant, which mankind could not keep.

God made a **unilateral** covenant with us in the New Covenant. In it, Jesus has already paid for us in His blood which He shed on the **cross**. Those who follow Jesus the Christ the Messiah inherit blessing rather than earn it. We have no action to perform to gain **salvation**. Our obedience is not a requirement for blessing, it is a response to being **loved**. We are **part of His family** in Christ, and He empowers us to obey by **grace through faith**.

He also empowers Christians to be His **ambassadors** so that we can tell the **gospel**, the good news of salvation, to others so that they can enter into His kingdom.

The main benefit He gives us is the means and opportunity to know Him as a **member of His family**. We can get to know Him in many ways, including by learning and studying **His names**.

His **name** is above every name, and the demons tremble at the name of Jesus. In fact, Christians can bind the devil in Jesus name by saying, "I bind up the devil bothering me in Jesus" name and cast it away from me." It is as if a spiritual rope or force stops the action of that demon, and then moves the enemy away from you. This stopping of demonic activity is part of **spiritual warfare**, which is important to learn and more fully described in my book *Discipling Muslim Background Believers*.

With an understanding of reading the Bible, prayer, God's covenant promises, His name, and spiritual warfare, it is appropriate to cover some more basics of Christianity.

6 SOME MORE BASICS OF CHRISTIANITY, INCLUDING EVANGELISM

God is our **Father**. Christians are **adopted into His family**, which is a very good thing. The ancient Roman custom of adoption is the reference for adoption into God's family. Romans could not disown an adopted child, just as God will not disown those that are His (Romans8:38-39). Christians are all adopted, and share in the inheritance with the firstborn, Jesus.

John 17 speaks of Jesus living in Christians, and the Father being in Jesus – therefore being in us. It also says we are in the Father. The Holy Spirit also indwells Christians. This means that **Christians are indwelt by the Father, Son and the Holy Spirit** – the **Trinity**. God resides in us – that is how close He wishes to be. It is easy to respond to Him when you can see such depths of love. This **intimacy** makes it easier to get to know and obey Him.

Christians obey, but the motive for that obedience comes from our relationship with God, not following rules to please Him. We already please Him. We are no longer slaves, but **friends** (John 15:15). Even better, we are sons and daughters (Romans 8:15-16). We are **fully loved**, and intimately know our **Father**.

We need faith to understand the above concept. **Faith** is being persuaded about God. With faith, we have the substance of the things that God causes us to hope for as we read about His promises in the Bible, and the evidence of things not seen. We can know that we are going to **heaven when we die**. We can also believe that at the end of time, **Jesus will return**, and we will **live with Him forever in heaven**.

As we grow in the knowledge of God, we will increase our ability to **keep our faith pure**, free of **syncretism** – the addition of practices and beliefs from other religions and belief systems.

One of the ways to keep faith pure is to make it a habit to focus on God through pursuing **spiritual disciplines**:

1. **Prayer**.
2. Setting aside time in solitude to **listen to God**.
3. **Worship** – verbally ascribing worth to God. The book of Psalms is filled with examples. Can be done individually or in small or large groups. It can be spoken, song, or even silent awe.
4. **Reading and studying the Bible**.
5. **Meditating on God's word**.
6. **Fasting**.
7. **Evangelism**. This is something to which every Christian is called to some degree, and can be done

intentionally and at the same time directed by God. It may or may not occur regularly because it should occur as the Lord leads. It is good to always intend to and be ready to share the gospel, the good news about Jesus Christ the Messiah and the salvation that comes through following Him as Lord and Savior. Please read the relevant sections of *Discipling Muslim Background Believers* for more information and instruction.

8. **Serving others**, especially those most in need.
9. **Tithing** and **giving**.

7 THE FOUNDATIONAL TEACHINGS

In the book of Hebrews, the writer speaks of foundational teachings that need to be learned before learning about righteousness, which is considered solid food while the others, though useful, are like milk – basic food.

> [11] About him [Jesus] we have many words to say, and hard to interpret, seeing you have become dull of hearing. [12] For although by this time you should be teachers, you again need to have someone teach you the rudiments of the first principles of the revelations of God. You have come to need milk, and not solid food. [13] For everyone who lives on milk is not experienced in the word of righteousness, for he is a baby. [14] But solid food is for those who are full grown, who by reason of use have their senses exercised to discern good and evil. **6** Therefore leaving the teaching of the first principles of Christ, let us press on to perfection—not laying again a foundation of repentance from dead works, of faith toward God, [2] of the teaching of baptisms, of laying on of hands, of resurrection of the dead, and of eternal judgment. Hebrews 5:11-6:2 WEB

These teachings will be summarized below.

7.1 REPENTANCE FROM DEAD WORKS

Repentance, in this context, means turning from sin and turning towards God. **Dead works** are those not based on **faith**. They may seem to be good things, but they have no value. They are most often done trying to please a God who is already so pleased with us that He died for us so that we can be free from death. Dead works are often **legalistic**. Thus, **repentance from dead works** means to turn away from doing things that are not from faith and that He has not asked for in order to try to please God.

7.2 FAITH TOWARDS GOD

Faith means to be persuaded about God. It is relational in that it is being persuaded not about a thing or series of facts about God, but about God to Whom you wish to relate. How you relate and the quality of your relationship will be affected by your persuasion about Him. Faith comes by **hearing**, and that hearing comes through **knowing God's word** (Romans 10:17). Faith also introduces us to **grace** (Romans 5:1-2), which **saves** us (Ephesians 2:4-10). Faith is accompanied by works (James 2:17-26).

7.3 INSTRUCTION ABOUT WASHINGS (BAPTISMS)

Baptism is one of the sacraments – an outward sign of an inward grace. In the Protestant church there are two sacraments: water baptism and **communion**.

Baptism means to immerse or dip under. The Bible describes two types: with water and **with the Holy Spirit**.

7.3.1 WATER BAPTISM

Water baptism is an outward symbol of an inward **grace**. The inward grace comes when, after **salvation**, Christians identify with Jesus Christ the Messiah's **death** and **resurrection** by being briefly immersed in water (signifying identifying with His death), and then being lifted up out of the water (signifying identifying with His resurrection and life). The grace spoken of is indicated in 1 Peter 3:21, which states that baptism is an appeal to God for a clean conscience. Note that this is not the same as salvation. A good conscience has more to do with the soul than the spirit – it has to do with removal of shame, the sense that we are not measuring up. Salvation gives us a **new spirit** and a **new nature**. Baptism is a further identification with Jesus' resurrection, and is not a vital part of salvation. It is very important and is necessary for

Christians. It need only be done once, and must be after salvation. The person being baptized should understand the significance of baptism.

Before a person is baptized, the baptizer should ask the person if they believe in and follow Jesus Christ the Messiah as Lord and Savior.

Christians are to be baptized in the name of the Father, Son and Holy Spirit. People doing baptisms should say something to the effect of the following:

> I baptize you in the name of the Father and the Son and the Holy Spirit. You are buried with Him in death (briefly immersing the person at this point), and raised with Him in newness of life (and raising the person out of the water while saying "and raised …").

The people being baptized should be dressed in a way to protect their dignity but not make it dangerous to be in the water, and have a change of clothes with them and preferably a private place to change in once baptized.

Christians can baptize another Christian. The person baptizing need not be an ordained minister – the Bible does not specify that an ordained minister does it.

7.3.2 <u>BAPTISM OF THE HOLY SPIRIT</u>

The above section describes the outpouring, or **baptism, of the Holy Spirit**. There are some important characteristics:

1. It is for people who are already Christians – already **saved**.
2. It can happen to the same person more than once.
3. It **empowers** for **service**.
4. Someone else usually prays for it with the **laying on of hands**. This means it can be requested.
5. There is some accompanying outward **manifestation of the Holy Spirit**.

7.4 LAYING ON OF HANDS

Laying on of hands is **praying** while touching the person you are praying for. The touch is discreet and light, and the person being prayed for usually requests this type of prayer. It is often done while praying for healing as well as for **appointing leaders** of any type, including of **small groups** and **churches**. It usually involves impartation of **anointing**, which is the transfer of spiritual power from God, through another, to the person being prayed for. The person praying acts almost like a conduit, and does not lose nor diminish any anointing on their own life.

7.5   RESURRECTION OF THE DEAD

God made people with eternal spirits. He originally wanted to have a relationship with them, but they chose against Him. Rather than throw people away, He sent Jesus, God in the flesh, to be an eternal sacrifice for our sins, once for all. He gave people an opportunity to be members of His family. They only had to repent and choose to follow Jesus Christ the Messiah as Lord and Savior. If they did so, they received a **new nature** and became part of God's family. They became **Christians**.

Those that are Christians when they die go to be with God forever. They will be resurrected with new bodies from the dead. Those who do not will go into the lake of fire with Satan and his fallen angels in hell.

7.6   ETERNAL JUDGMENT

As stated above, those who die as Christians will be **safe from eternal judgment** for their sins because Jesus Christ paid for them, whereas those who are not Christians will go into the lake of fire with Satan and his fallen angels in hell.

8 RIGHTEOUSNESS

As stated in the last chapter, the solid food of **righteousness** is for the mature Christian – the one who already knows the things in the chapters above, especially the chapter immediately above on the foundational teachings.

God is a king and a judge. We cannot approach Him on our terms, only on His. He requires that those who approach Him are spiritually clean through and through, not just on the surface. We must also have a **relationship with Him**, which gives us the right to approach Him. Please note that many people can enter a courtroom, but the judge only calls to himself those that he recognizes as having standing with him – a proper relationship with the court. Righteousness is a Christian's good legal standing before God in Christ. The only way to obtain that standing is through **being in Christ**, which means following Jesus Christ the Messiah as Lord and Savior – **salvation**. Those that do have standing to approach God, to be **part of His family**, to **know Him**, and to **converse and relate to the God of all**.

[17] Therefore if anyone is in Christ, he is a new creation. The old things have passed away. Behold, all things have become new. [18] But all things are of God, who reconciled us to himself through Jesus Christ, and gave

to us the ministry of reconciliation; [19] namely, that God was in Christ reconciling the world to himself, not reckoning to them their trespasses, and having committed to us the word of reconciliation. [20] We are therefore ambassadors on behalf of Christ, as though God were entreating by us: we beg you on behalf of Christ, be reconciled to God. [21] For him who knew no sin he made to be sin on our behalf; so that in him we might become the righteousness of God. 2 Corinthians 5:17-21 WEB

Like convicted criminals in a courtroom awaiting sentencing, we were guilty before God and deserved the death penalty. We could appear before God who loves us at all times, but not for a good relationship – only for sentencing. He could hear and answer our prayers, but the sentence would not change – we had and have all broken at least a part of His law, so the sentence was and is death. Then Jesus came, paid our penalty and gave us life through His **death** and **resurrection**. In Christ, **new things have come and the old has passed away**. In Christ, we are neither criminals nor are we the accused. We are free and have good standing before God – we are righteous.

Please notice that verse 21 says that we become God's righteousness after salvation. That means we are righteous by nature, just as God is righteous. We are a new creation (2

Corinthians 5:21), and the old has passed away. Righteousness is not a legalistic avoidance of bad things but rather a legal position that is based on relationship with God. We are given a **new nature** – one that wants to obey and please God. We still have the ability to sin, but must choose sin. This is a drastic difference from before, when we sinned by nature.

Righteousness is not earned by us. Our righteousness was purchased for us by Jesus Christ, our savior. We **receive** it as a gift. Much like in a court, in which a judge grants standing, righteousness is granted to us if we follow Jesus Christ the Messiah as Lord and Savior. We have to receive it, meaning that it is given to us and we must accept it, much as we reach out and accept an offered gift. This is a gift we receive with the heart.

> [17] For if by the trespass of the one, death reigned through the one; so much more will those who receive the abundance of grace and of the gift of righteousness reign in life through the one, Jesus Christ. Romans 5:17 WEB

God gives us righteousness as a gift when we follow Jesus Christ the Messiah as Lord and Savior. Righteousness is standing to be with Him and properly relate to Him, and He gives it in abundance. We simply **receive** it gladly and thankfully.

9 RELATIONSHIP WITH GOD (BASED ON A UNILATERAL COVENANT)

The relationship between God and Christians is based on His **unilateral covenant**. The benefits are much like an inheritance from Jesus. He died, and we receive benefits. Among the things we **receive** are:

1. Freedom from **sin**;
2. **Salvation** makes us **new creations**, able to properly relate to God, and **enter into His family**;
3. God's **righteousness**; and
4. Best of all, a relationship with God that is eternal (John 17:3 and 1 John 5:20).

As part of that relationship, **God gives us purpose**. We have the privilege to work with Him in His kingdom, and He gives us a good **plan for our lives**.

[10] For we are his workmanship, created in Christ Jesus for good works, which God prepared before that we would walk in them. Ephesians 2:10 WEB

Now that's an inheritance!

9.1 UNDERSTANDING RIGHTEOUSNESS

Understanding **righteousness** is a key to understanding how to live as a Christian. This understanding allows us to see who we are in Christ, how to walk by **grace through faith**, and how to avoid the trap of trying to live in our own strength. We could not live in our own strength to begin with – that is why Jesus Christ the Messiah had to die for us and be **resurrected**.

Through Jesus' **death** and resurrection, those who follow Him as Lord are new creations. They have new natures, and the old is gone. They are brand new. In fact, they are born again of God's word (1 Peter 1:23).

It is common knowledge that a seed produces after its kind – orange seeds produce oranges and grape seeds produce grapes. The seed that a Christian is produced from is the word of God. **Salvation** gives us a new nature, which is divine (2 Peter 1:4) because God's word is divine.

Christians become the righteousness of God, meaning that they have perfect legal standing before God.

[17] Therefore if anyone is in Christ, he is a new creation. The old things have passed away. Behold, all things have become new. [18] But all things are of God, who reconciled us to himself through Jesus Christ, and gave

to us the ministry of reconciliation; [19] namely, that God was in Christ reconciling the world to himself, not reckoning to them their trespasses, and having committed to us the word of reconciliation. [20] We are therefore ambassadors on behalf of Christ, as though God were entreating by us: we beg you on behalf of Christ, be reconciled to God. [21] For him who knew no sin he made to be sin on our behalf; so that in him we might become the righteousness of God. 2 Corinthians 5:17-21 WEB

This righteousness is not imputed righteousness, in which we are simply counted righteous because of Jesus. It is way better. We actually *become* righteous (*see* verse 21 above) – and it gets even better still. It's actually mind-blowing in its beauty. Because of the finished work of the **cross**, **resurrection** and being in Him, the righteousness we become is the *righteousness of God*. We are certainly not Him, or His equal, but we do have His standing. We are as righteous as He is, because He made it that way. It is like going into the Supreme Court and having the same standing as the Chief Justice. There is none better. No wonder there is no condemnation – there *cannot* be any. No one in His court can sustain an accusation against us because we have His standing.

There is therefore now no condemnation to those who are in Christ Jesus, who don't walk according to the flesh, but according to the Spirit. Romans 8:1 WEB

Knowing and understanding this righteousness helps in many ways, including dealing with fear, insecurity and inadequacy. When you understand that God did everything He did to get you back from sin and death, then you will also know that that is the extent to which the Most High God went for you, that He will never leave you, that He will always help you, and that He will always be for you. This understanding helps remove fear because we know we are secure in Him. We can enjoy **completely confident living**.

Understanding that He chose us to always be with Him in right standing, based not on our works but Jesus', helps us know our value, thus minimizing insecurity.

Understanding that we are righteous new creations and that He is at work in and through us helps us know that **our adequacy is from Him**, removing any sense of inadequacy.

9.2   WHAT IS OBEDIENCE?

Obedience is doing what another orders or requests, and being under their authority. Some characteristics of Christian obedience include:

1. It is relational, meaning that it is in response to being loved by God (not doing right things for wrong reasons, including legalism - seeking the approval that you already have in Christ – or seeking man's approval);
2. It is whole-hearted;
3. It is complete;
4. It is timely; and
5. It is cheerful, without complaint or grumbling.

Obedience involves submitting to God's **lordship**. It also involves **loving others**. Please note that His commandments are not a burden.

[1] Whoever believes that Jesus is the Christ has been born of God. Whoever loves the Father also loves the child who is born of him. [2] By this we know that we love the children of God, when we love God and keep his commandments. [3] For this is the love of God, that we keep his commandments. His commandments are not grievous. [4] For whatever is born of God overcomes the world. This is the victory that has overcome the world: your faith. 1 John 5:1-4 WEB

Also, **His yoke is easy and burden is light**.

9.2.1   SEEKING FIRST HIS KINGDOM AND HIS RIGHTEOUSNESS

Part of understanding righteousness is to seek first His kingdom and His righteousness. God sets seeking His Kingdom and His **righteousness** as a priority. It is part of seeking Him – our first priority.

> [31] "Therefore don't be anxious, saying, 'What will we eat?', 'What will we drink?' or, 'With what will we be clothed?' [32] For the Gentiles seek after all these things; for your heavenly Father knows that you need all these things. [33] But seek first God's Kingdom, and his righteousness; and all these things will be given to you as well. [34] Therefore don't be anxious for tomorrow, for tomorrow will be anxious for itself. Each day's own evil is sufficient. Matthew 6:31-34 WEB

A kingdom is usually the geographical territory over which a king exercises his authority. It is where things occur according to the way the king wants them to happen. In the case of God's kingdom, **it is not only a place but also the hearts of people**.

Righteousness means having good legal standing before God. It comes through a proper relationship with God rather than our efforts. To seek His righteousness would mean to live out the life He has given us by **grace through faith**.

Verse 33 indicates that we should put seeking God's kingdom and His righteousness above seeking our own basic needs, but not because it causes God to provide for us. To think that is to belittle the generous nature of God. He's not making deals, He's giving us the assurance that He knows our needs and will take care of us. We can rest and put our primary focus on God and serving others. Please note that God does not prohibit seeking to meet our own needs. He's focused on our prioritization of things that He values.

Living according to God's ways is actually easy when compared with the alternative, living according to our own standards – which by definition is legalism. God calls us to walk in His truth. That usually means that we follow a fairly narrow way. To me, living out the life God has put in me is much easier than legalism, which involves doing and avoiding thousands of things. God makes life simple for us, saying, "Follow Me!" rather than letting me defend my life against breaking a law – which would result in my death. It is simple because I focus on one thing, following Him, rather than trying to avoid those thousands of things.

9.3   INTIMACY WITH GOD

Intimacy in the context of our relationship with God means relational closeness. For Christians, God calls us friends (John 15:15). This in no way brings God down, nor does it take away the need to **fear Him**. Christians must still obey – He is God.

Christians can know God in a very close way. He brings us up to a level where we can be family through **salvation** in Jesus Christ the Messiah, His Son. We are adopted into His family, and can call Him "Abba". This is much the same as the English word "Daddy". It speaks of the closeness that God wishes to have with us.

> [15] For you didn't receive the spirit of bondage again to fear, but you received the Spirit of adoption, by whom we cry, "Abba! Father!"
> [16] The Spirit himself testifies with our spirit that we are children of God; [17] and if children, then heirs; heirs of God, and joint heirs with Christ; if indeed we suffer with him, that we may also be glorified with him. [18] For I consider that the sufferings of this present time are not worthy to be compared with the glory which will be revealed toward us. Romans 8:15-18 WEB

Galatians 4:1-7 is also a verse that is important to know regarding this topic. It also speaks of being part of His family.

Please note that the ancient Roman custom of adoption is being referred to in the verses above. Romans could not disown an adopted child, just as God will not disown those that are His (Romans8:38-39). Christians are all adopted, and because of salvation we share in the inheritance with the firstborn, Jesus.

John 17 speaks of Jesus living in Christians, and the Father being in Jesus – therefore being in us. It also says we are in the Father. The **Holy Spirit** also indwells Christians. This means that Christians are indwelt by the Father, Son and the Holy Spirit. God resides in us – that is how close He wishes to be. It is easy to respond to Him when you can see such depths of love. This **intimacy** makes it easier to get to know and obey Him.

Christians must obey, but the motive for that obedience comes from our relationship with God, not a desire to follow rules to please Him. We already please Him. We are no longer slaves, but friends (John 15:15). Even better, we are sons and daughters (Romans 8:15-16). We are fully loved, and can intimately know our **Father**.

9.3.1   RELATIONAL, NOT LEGALISTIC

A Christian's relationship with God is like that of a family member to a good father. There are rules to the house. The family members follow them not out of fear that they will not be loved or that they will be kicked out of the house, but rather because they love the one who made the rules and want to obey as part of that love.

Similarly, Christians know that God loves them and values people so much that He gave Jesus Christ the Messiah to die in mankind's place. People that follow Jesus Christ the Messiah as Lord and Savior experience **salvation** and obey God because of the relationship, not just to follow rules and commands. Simply following rules and commands is legalistic. Christians follow and obey because of a relationship – one with their loving Father. In fact, the word is closer in the original to "Abba", which is what many little children call their fathers. The name signifies the love, closeness and care that God has for us.

Obeying still takes effort, and the power for that relational obedience comes by **grace through faith**. This type of living leads to freedom in Christ.

9.3.2   <u>FREEDOM IN CHRIST</u>

In Christ, Christians are free. In fact, freedom for us was His goal.

> Stand firm therefore in the liberty by which Christ has made us free, and don't be entangled again with a yoke of bondage.   Galatians 5:1 WEB

That does not mean we are completely unrestrained. Completely unrestrained individual freedom does not work in a society.

9.3.2.1   <u>TRUE FREEDOM NEEDS CONSTRAINTS</u>

The word "freedom" seems to suggest that we can do as we please. I suggest that we are actually freer when some constraint is put onto our freedom.

It is true that Christ set us free for freedom:

> Stand firm therefore in the liberty by which Christ has made us free, and don't be entangled again with a yoke of bondage. Galatians 5:1 WEB

Paul is talking about freedom from legalism. He also mentions that our freedom is constrained:

> [14] For the love of Christ constrains us; because we judge thus, that one died for all, therefore all died. [15] He died for all, that those who live should no longer live to themselves, but to him who for their sakes died and rose again. 2 Corinthians 5:14-15 WEB

In Greek, the word "controls" in verse 14 means "constrains" in the sense of pressing in and closing off choices.

Verses 14-15 indicate that because Jesus died for us all, we all died and we no longer live for ourselves but for Him.

Thus, we are constrained to love Him and people, and conduct ourselves accordingly. I think that this constraint improves our freedom in that it works better than unbridled individualism. When we commit to love others, we actually gain, though that gain is not our motive – knowing and obeying Him is our motive. Rather than striving to take at the expense of others (a zero-sum game), we then give and serve to bless others. This giving and serving recognizes our interdependence with others and our dependence on God. It also recognizes that our lot and freedom get better as the situation around us improves. Love improves the situation around us, while unbridled individualism ultimately tears it down.

9.3.2.2 AN EASY YOKE AND A LIGHT BURDEN

Jesus said His yoke was easy and His burden was light in Matthew 11:

25 At that time Jesus said, "I praise You, Father, Lord of heaven and earth, that You have hidden these things from *the* wise and intelligent and have revealed them to infants. 26 25 At that time, Jesus answered, "I thank you, Father, Lord of heaven and earth, that you hid these things from the wise and understanding, and revealed them to infants. 26 Yes, Father, for so it was well-pleasing in your sight. 27 All things have been delivered to me by my Father. No one knows the Son, except the Father; neither does anyone know the Father, except the Son, and he to whom the Son desires to reveal him. 28 "Come to me, all you who labor and are heavily burdened, and I will give you rest. 29 Take my yoke upon you, and learn from me, for I am gentle and humble in heart; and you will find rest for your souls. 30 For my yoke is easy, and my burden is light." Matthew 11:25-30 WEB

One can wonder how this can be, especially in light of the imprisonment, beatings, persecution and suffering of the disciples. That does not sound easy, and seems to set up a conflict between experience and the passage. I think resolution of that conflict comes from looking at the passage again. The next five sections do that.

9.3.2.2.1 REVELATION IS NOT BASED ON HUMAN WISDOM OR INTELLIGENCE

In Matthew 11:25, Jesus says that the wise and intelligent were prevented from seeing things that were revealed to infants – who possess several good qualities, including humility and being learners.

In verse 27, Jesus speaks of the knowledge that the Father and Son have about each other. They have a very intimate relationship, and Jesus chooses who gets to know the Father. To allow them into the relationship, He reveals the Father to them.

9.3.2.2.2 REST FOR THE WEARY AND HEAVY-LADEN

Verse 28 contains Jesus' famous invitation to the weary and heavy-laden to come to Him, saying that He will give them rest. Note that this invitation is in context of Jesus choosing who to reveal the Father to. The weary and heavy-laden tend to be willing to receive and walk in humility. (Please note that the weary and heavy laden are not the only ones who receive revelation of the Father.)

9.3.2.2.3 AN EASY YOKE AND A LIGHT BURDEN

The yoke is Jesus' **lordship**. He is master, but serving Him is easier than any alternative. Note that Jesus' invitation to take His yoke involves learning from Him *because* He is meek and humble in heart, and because we will find rest for our souls.

Jesus is easy to learn from because of His character, and His humility means that the burden is light. The end result is being with Him in heaven, and **Jesus is the only way to salvation**.

9.3.2.2.4 INTERNAL REST MAKES EVERYTHING EASIER

Knowing about salvation still does not completely resolve the conflict between "easy" and the conflict and turmoil of life, but it gets us closer. We can see that Jesus chooses who knows the Father, and those who are weary and heavy-laden that come to Him and become His disciples find rest for their souls. Rest inside is great, but how does that help deal with the difficult things in life?

Easy is a relative word. Living with Him, under any circumstances, is easier than living without Him because of the internal rest – which gives us peace in the midst of all circumstances. Taking Jesus yoke gives us confidence to live, and the ability to deal with problems through **grace**. We also have a refuge, and someone to turn to for help – the King of the Universe who loves us. If we mess up, **He restores us**.

9.3.2.2.5 SELF-FOCUS INCREASES PAIN

The disciples spoke of their struggles, but seemed to say that they were still encouraged and hopeful in the midst of the pain. I think it was because they were not holding onto their own lives. Holding onto our own lives – self-focus – magnifies pain because then we are always conscious of the pain.

The way to deal with that magnification is to repent of pride and self-pity, then look to Him. He is an ever-present help in times of trouble. Let go of your life by giving it to Him. He cares for you, and will take care of you. He even heals pain.

The internal rest offered by taking Jesus' yoke gives us peace and rest in our souls and help in times of difficulty. That is certainly easier than doing things without Him. There is then no conflict between our circumstances and the passage because we have what we need in Christ to deal with life.

10 GOD KEEPS HIS PROMISES

God is faithful, and keeps His promises. It is a part of His nature to do so. He gives **promises** to us so that we can know Him and fulfill His commands by **grace through faith**.

10.1 SOME OF GOD'S PROMISES

Below are some of God's promises. Note that some of them require something from you. The headings are categories that make finding relevant promises easier to find.

Please also note that there are many others, and God can apply them to you. Ask God to show you through His word what He is saying to you for your circumstances or even your life. While many promises are generally for Christians, He will make you pay special attention to certain verses that will tell of the things He will do in your life. Do not try to pick something that seems good to you. Let Him lead you to the verses he has for your life. Memorize them so that you can refer to them in your mind at any time.

10.1.1 FORGIVENESS

[9] If we confess our sins, he is faithful and righteous to forgive us the sins, and to cleanse us from all unrighteousness.   1 John 1:9 WEB

10.1.2 SALVATION

[9] that if you will confess with your mouth that Jesus is Lord, and believe in your heart that God raised him from the dead, you will be saved. [10] For with the heart, one believes unto righteousness; and with the mouth confession is made unto salvation.   Romans 10:9-10 WEB

10.1.3 RIGHTEOUSNESS

[17] Therefore if anyone is in Christ, he is a new creation. The old things have passed away. Behold, all things have become new. [18] But all things are of God, who reconciled us to himself through Jesus Christ, and gave to us the ministry of reconciliation; [19] namely, that God was in Christ reconciling the world to himself, not reckoning to them their trespasses, and having committed to us the word of reconciliation. [20] We are

therefore ambassadors on behalf of Christ, as though God were entreating by us: we beg you on behalf of Christ, be reconciled to God. [21] For him who knew no sin he made to be sin on our behalf; so that in him we might become the righteousness of God. 2 Corinthians 5:17-21 WEB

10.1.4 FREEDOM

[31] Jesus therefore said to those Jews who had believed him, "If you remain in my word, then you are truly my disciples. [32] You will know the truth, and the truth will make you free." John 8:31-32 WEB

10.1.5 LOVE

[8] For I am persuaded, that neither death, nor life, nor angels, nor principalities, nor things present, nor things to come, nor powers, [39] nor height, nor depth, nor any other created thing, will be able to separate us from the love of God, which is in Christ Jesus our Lord. Romans 8:38-39 WEB

[31] What then shall we say about these things? If God is for us, who can be against us? Romans 8:31 WEB

10.1.6 <u>PROVISION</u>

[31] "Therefore don't be anxious, saying, 'What will we eat?', 'What will we drink?' or, 'With what will we be clothed?' [32] For the Gentiles seek after all these things; for your heavenly Father knows that you need all these things. [33] But seek first God's Kingdom, and his righteousness; and all these things will be given to you as well. Matthew 6:31-33 WEB

[19] My God will supply every need of yours according to his riches in glory in Christ Jesus. Philippians 4:19 WEB

[10] Bring the whole tithe into the storehouse, that there may be food in my house, and test me now in this," says Yahweh of Armies, "if I will not open you the windows of heaven, and pour you out a blessing, that there will not be room enough for.   Malachi 3:10 WEB

10.1.7 GOD'S PLAN FOR YOU

11 For I know the thoughts that I think toward you, says
Yahweh, thoughts of peace, and not of evil, to give you
hope and a future.   Jeremiah 29:11 WEB

5 Trust in Yahweh with all your heart,
   and don't lean on your own understanding.
6 In all your ways acknowledge him,
   and he will make your paths straight. Proverbs 3:5-6
WEB

10.1.8 PERFECT PEACE

3 You will keep whoever's mind is steadfast in perfect
peace,
   because he trusts in you. Isaiah 26:3 WEB

10.1.9 GOOD RESULTS OF WAITING ON THE LORD

29 He gives power to the weak.
   He increases the strength of him who has no might.
30 Even the youths faint and get weary,
   and the young men utterly fall;
31   But those who wait for Yahweh will renew their

strength.

They will mount up with wings like eagles.

They will run, and not be weary.

They will walk, and not faint. Isaiah 40:29-31 WEB

10.1.10   PRAYER

[7] "Ask, and it will be given you. Seek, and you will find. Knock, and it will be opened for you. Matthew 7:7 WEB

Please note that the verbs in the original language of the Bible in the above verse indicate that you should keep doing the verb. So, ask and keep asking; seek and keep seeking; and knock and keep knocking.

[6] In nothing be anxious, but in everything, by prayer and petition with thanksgiving, let your requests be made known to God. [7] And the peace of God, which surpasses all understanding, will guard your hearts and your thoughts in Christ Jesus. Philippians 4:6-7 WEB

10.1.11   GOD GIVES WISDOM TO THOSE WHO ASK

[5] But if any of you lacks wisdom, let him ask of God, who gives to all liberally and without reproach; and it will be given to him. James 1:5 WEB

10.1.11.1.1   ANOINTING

[1] The Lord Yahweh's Spirit is on me;

because Yahweh has anointed me to preach good news to the humble.

He has sent me to bind up the broken hearted,

to proclaim liberty to the captives,

and release to those who are bound;

[2] to proclaim the year of Yahweh's favor,

and the day of vengeance of our God;

to comfort all who mourn;

[3] to provide for those who mourn in Zion,

to give to them a garland for ashes,

the oil of joy for mourning,

the garment of praise for the spirit of heaviness;

that they may be called trees of righteousness,

the planting of Yahweh,

that he may be glorified.

[4] They will rebuild the old ruins.

They will raise up the places long devastated.

They will repair the ruined cities,

that have been devastated for many generations.

⁵ Strangers will stand and feed your flocks,

and foreigners will work your fields and your

vineyards.

⁶ But you will be called Yahweh's priests.

Men will call you the servants of our God.

You will eat the wealth of the nations,

and you will boast in their glory.

⁷ Instead of your shame you will have double.

Instead of dishonor, they will rejoice in their portion.

Therefore in their land, they will possess double.

Everlasting joy will be to them. Isaiah 61:1-7 WEB

10.1.12   PROTECTION

¹⁷ No weapon that is formed against you will prevail;

and you will condemn every tongue that rises against

you in judgment.

This is the heritage of Yahweh's servants,

and their righteousness is of me," says Yahweh.

Isaiah 54:17 WEB

[1] I will lift up my eyes to the hills.

Where does my help come from?

[2] My help comes from Yahweh,

who made heaven and earth.

[3] He will not allow your foot to be moved.

He who keeps you will not slumber.

[4] Behold, he who keeps Israel

will neither slumber nor sleep.

[5] Yahweh is your keeper.

Yahweh is your shade on your right hand.

[6] The sun will not harm you by day,

nor the moon by night.

[7] Yahweh will keep you from all evil.

He will keep your soul.

[8] Yahweh will keep your going out and your coming in,

from this time forward, and forever more. Psalm 121

WEB

[1] He who dwells in the secret place of the Most High

will rest in the shadow of the Almighty.

[2] I will say of Yahweh, "He is my refuge and my
fortress;

my God, in whom I trust."

[3] For he will deliver you from the snare of the fowler,

and from the deadly pestilence.

⁴ He will cover you with his feathers.

   Under his wings you will take refuge.

   His faithfulness is your shield and rampart.

⁵ You shall not be afraid of the terror by night,

   nor of the arrow that flies by day;

⁶   nor of the pestilence that walks in darkness,

   nor of the destruction that wastes at noonday.

⁷ A thousand may fall at your side,

   and ten thousand at your right hand;

   but it will not come near you.

⁸ You will only look with your eyes,

   and see the recompense of the wicked.

⁹ Because you have made Yahweh your refuge,

   and the Most High your dwelling place,

¹⁰ no evil shall happen to you,

   neither shall any plague come near your dwelling.

¹¹ For he will put his angels in charge of you,

   to guard you in all your ways.

¹² They will bear you up in their hands,

   so that you won't dash your foot against a stone.

¹³ You will tread on the lion and cobra.

   You will trample the young lion and the serpent
underfoot.

¹⁴ "Because he has set his love on me, therefore I will
deliver him.

I will set him on high, because he has known my
name.

15 He will call on me, and I will answer him.

I will be with him in trouble.

I will deliver him, and honor him.

16 I will satisfy him with long life,

and show him my salvation." Psalm 91 WEB

2 When you pass through the waters, I will be with you;

and through the rivers, they will not overflow you.

When you walk through the fire, you will not be burned,

and flame will not scorch you. Isaiah 43:2 WEB

14 Yahweh will fight for you, and you shall be still."
Exodus 14:14 WEB

The implication in the verse above is that He fights while we
stay still – we do not have to do anything. This only happens at
rare intervals, so fight unless He tells you to be still.

7 Be subject therefore to God. But resist the devil, and he
will flee from you. James 4:7 WEB

10.1.13   <u>JESUS IS ALWAYS WITH US</u>

Jesus is always with us.

> [20] teaching them to observe all things that I commanded you. Behold, I am with you always, even to the end of the age." Amen. Matthew 28:20 WEB

11 GOD CARES FOR YOU

God is love (1 John 4:8). When a Christian meditates on **who God is** as well as the **names of God**, that care becomes evident. Please also see the section below regarding **how God sees you**.

12 INTIMACY WITH GOD

Christians can have a very close relationship with God. It is pure and intimate in the way a good father is intimate with a small child that he loves very much. Some of it has been covered already in Chapter 9.3 above, called **Intimacy with God**. Please note that the reference points to both the chapter above and also to my book *Discipling Muslim Background Believers*.

To have an intimate relationship with God, it is very helpful to know how God sees you.

12.1 HOW GOD SEES YOU

If you wonder how God sees you, the Bible has much to say. As a Christian, you are a member of His family, are deeply loved, and have God living inside of you. He loves you the same as He loves Jesus, His Son (John 17:23).

12.1.1 GOD IS LIVING IN YOU AND YOU ARE PART OF HIS FAMILY

When you read the verses below, please keep in mind that **Jesus** is the fulness of the godhead, the **Trinity** – Father, Son and Holy Spirit.

[20] Not for these only do I pray, but for those also who believe in me through their word, [21] that they may all be one; even as you, Father, are in me, and I in you, that they also may be one in us; that the world may believe that you sent me. [22] The glory which you have given me, I have given to them; that they may be one, even as we are one; [23] I in them, and you in me, that they may be perfected into one; that the world may know that you sent me, and loved them, even as you loved me. [24] Father, I desire that they also whom you have given me be with me where I am, that they may see my glory, which you have given me, for you loved me before the foundation of the world. [25] Righteous Father, the world hasn't known you, but I knew you; and these knew that you sent me. [26] I made known to them your name, and will make it known; that the love with which you loved me may be in them, and I in them." John 17:20-26 WEB

Christians are in God, and God lives in them. The only way this happens is through **salvation**.

You have perfect legal standing with God. You are completely **forgiven** and have a **new nature**. When you **sin**, you can ask for forgiveness after **repenting**. God sees you as **part of His family**. Jesus is in you. You have a new nature, and He sees that too.

God calls Christians a royal priesthood and a holy nation.

> [9] But you are a chosen race, a royal priesthood, a holy nation, a people for God's own possession, that you may proclaim the excellence of him who called you out of darkness into his marvelous light: [10] who in time past were no people, but now are God's people, who had not obtained mercy, but now have obtained mercy. 1 Peter 2:9-10 WEB

The word "royal" in the Greek suggests a group of kings. Christians share, under the headship of the Father, Son and Holy Spirit, a royal nature through Jesus Christ. It is part of our new nature. Thus, verse 9 is calling us kings, queens and priests. That is part of how God sees you.

Also, each Christian is part of God's chosen people, heirs to the promises given to Abraham and also to all the promises of the **new covenant** for His people. God also sees you as one who receives **mercy**.

God also views You as part of Him. A Christian is born of God, of His word.

> [23] having been born again, not of corruptible seed, but of incorruptible, through the word of God, which lives and remains forever. 1 Peter 1:23 WEB

We are not God, but He makes us sharers in His **resurrection** so that we can have His life.

> [5] For if we have become united with him in the likeness of his death, we will also be part of his resurrection; …. Romans 6:5 WEB

We can share in His resurrection life because he made us a **new creation**. When He sees us, He sees a beloved member of His family, who has a new nature and **perfect legal standing** to make requests, and who is indwelt by the Holy Spirit. He has a **good plan for** you and your life and will do good for you even in the midst of the worst circumstances. If you are a Christian, you already have the greatest gift that can ever be given, the ability to be part of the family of God and to know Him.

He also sees you as His deeply and completely loved masterpiece.

12.1.2 YOU ARE A COMPLETELY AND DEEPLY LOVED MASTERPIECE!

If you ever need encouragement about yourself or wonder how God thinks about you, one of the best things to consider is Psalm 139.

The Psalm is written by King David, who seems to be faced with a significant problem. Verses19-22 indicate that the ungodly are confronting David (probably to kill him), and that David has made God's enemies his enemies because of his love for God.

David is understandably anxious (verse 23). For encouragement, he remembers God's complete knowledge of him, love for him, and the way that God created him – a completely and deeply loved masterpiece.

The wonderful thing is that God feels the same way about each of as individuals. It's a great feeling knowing that each of us can legitimately put ourselves in David's shoes in this Psalm and ponder how much God loves us. Please also put yourself in his shoes as you read and reflect on the comments below the verses.

[1] Yahweh, you have searched me,
  and you know me.

75

² You know my sitting down and my rising up.

   You perceive my thoughts from afar.

³ You search out my path and my lying down,

   and are acquainted with all my ways.

⁴ For there is not a word on my tongue,

   but, behold, Yahweh, you know it altogether.

⁵ You hem me in behind and before.

   You laid your hand on me.

⁶ This knowledge is beyond me.

   It's lofty.

   I can't attain it.

⁷ Where could I go from your Spirit?

   Or where could I flee from your presence?

⁸ If I ascend up into heaven, you are there.

   If I make my bed in Sheol, behold, you are there!

⁹ If I take the wings of the dawn,

   and settle in the uttermost parts of the sea;

¹⁰ Even there your hand will lead me,

   and your right hand will hold me.

¹¹ If I say, "Surely the darkness will overwhelm me;

   the light around me will be night";

¹² even the darkness doesn't hide from you,

   but the night shines as the day.

   The darkness is like light to you.

¹³ For you formed my inmost being.

You knit me together in my mother's womb.

14 I will give thanks to you,

for I am fearfully and wonderfully made.

Your works are wonderful.

My soul knows that very well.

15 My frame wasn't hidden from you,

when I was made in secret,

woven together in the depths of the earth.

16 Your eyes saw my body.

In your book they were all written,

the days that were ordained for me,

when as yet there were none of them.

17 How precious to me are your thoughts, God!

How vast is their sum!

18 If I would count them, they are more in number than the sand.

When I wake up, I am still with you.

19 If only you, God, would kill the wicked.

Get away from me, you bloodthirsty men!

20 For they speak against you wickedly.

Your enemies take your name in vain.

21 Yahweh, don't I hate those who hate you?

Am I not grieved with those who rise up against you?

22 I hate them with perfect hatred.

They have become my enemies.

²³ Search me, God, and know my heart.

    Try me, and know my thoughts.

²⁴ See if there is any wicked way in me,

    and lead me in the everlasting way.. Psalm 139:1-24

WEB

Verse 1

This is the Lord that we are talking about. The one who made Heaven and Earth, sky, sun, moon and the universe. He is so high, so important, so powerful, yet He chooses to search and know (this word in Hebrew means know fully, completely and intimately) *me*. The reason is in verse 17 – He thinks of me many times, and I am precious to Him. He likes and loves me, and *wants to know and love me*.

Verse 2

God knows where I am and what I am doing in such great detail that He knows every time I sit down and get up. (He will never forget, either – He's God.) He wants to know what I am doing because He cares about me. He knows how I feel, and He understands and cares also about my feelings.

Verse 3

He doesn't just take a quick look at where I'm going. He scrutinizes it. He cares about every detail of my path. He also scrutinizes my lying down – presumably my sleeping. So, He scrutinizes what I do day and night, watching over me and being with me.

My ways are not just what I do. My ways involve my values, which effect (in the sense of produce and energize) my motives and intentions. These then produce and influence my actions. God is intimately familiar with that whole chain inside me. He wants to know it, because I am precious to Him.

Verse 4

Because He is God, He knows and cares about what I say before I even say it.

Verse 5

Enclosure here speaks of God's protection. He takes a personal interest in protecting me.

When God laid His hand on people in the Bible, it was to empower them to do specific tasks that were fulfilling for the person and that would bring great glory to God. That's what the last part of the fifth verse is saying He has done to me. He has a good purpose for my life, and what He plans will happen.

Verse 6

Basically, God's goodness to me is mind-blowing, and I cannot grasp it.

Verses 7-10
These verses say that God is everywhere, and even if I go astray or try to run from His plan, I will end up with Him and part of His plan. He will lead me always, and He is good.

Verses 11-12

God can always see, even when I am afraid and cannot see, when I am sure that circumstances will overwhelm me. He is there and will take care of me in all circumstances – they do not impede Him in any way.

Verse 13

God made my personality, thoughts, and my emotions. He made them the way He wanted them to be. He also put my body together inside my mother's womb, weaving it with His hands.

Verse 14

Considering the things in the last 13 verses, I have to stop and give thanks to God, because I am so very well made that I inspire people to be in awe of God. My soul knows that God made me well.

Verse 15

God hid me away in secret when He made me, away from the eyes of others. Yet my body was visible to Him. He hid me because I am special, the work of the Master – a masterpiece that He loves. Things that are common or lack value are neither hidden away nor made in secret by God, only the extra-special and ultra-valuable.

Verse 16

God saw what I looked like and knew what would happen in my entire life before I was born. He loved me so much that the story of my life was lovingly written into His book before I was born. Knowing all that I would do, good and bad, He loved me so much that I was born. He wanted me to have life, and He gave it to me. He loves me completely, knowing every part of me, inside and out.

Verses 17-18

God thinks precious thoughts about me; so many that they would outnumber the grains of sand. I am deeply loved. He is still watching over me when I wake up.

Verses 19-22

These verses describe David's situation, obviously a bad one. It seems that David had chosen to make God's enemies his own enemies, and they were probably trying to kill David. His thoughts, captured in this Psalm are not from a mountain top experience, but rather him remembering God's love for him. David knew what to think about in a time of great distress – God loves me, I am well made by God and have a God-given purpose that will be carried out.

Verses 23-24

Like David, I can ask God to search me (which David had said God had already done in verse 1, but David asked in

verse 23 with a different purpose – for correction and healing)
and experience my anxious thoughts. These thoughts were
from a thought pattern that was causing David pain. I can ask
God to see if there is a way in me that is causing me pain
("hurtful" is better translated "way of pain" and refers to
something that would be hurtful to David (or me)), to correct
and heal me and lead me in the everlasting way – meaning that I
follow Him.

Not only does this type of reflection reveal how deeply
loved we are, it can also show how God deals with anxiety,
corrects and heals us, and causes us to follow Him

12.1.3 HE SEES YOU HAVING THE WORTH OF HIS SON

An interesting and valid way to see how God sees the
worth of a human life is through the understanding that an
individual will pay what that individual feels the purchase is
worth. Otherwise, the person will not make the purchase. God
paid for us with His Son, an infinite price for each of us. He
willingly gave for each of us the maximum that He had.

[19] Or don't you know that your body is a temple of the
Holy Spirit which is in you, which you have from God?
You are not your own, [20] for you were bought with a

price. Therefore glorify God in your body and in your spirit, which are God's. 1 Corinthians 6:19-20 WEB

The payment of His Son shows the great love that God has for each and every person. We receive the benefit of His love and esteem fully only when we choose to receive Jesus' sacrifice as applying to us and **follow Jesus Christ the Messiah as Lord and Savior**.

God loved us so much that He gave us everything He had. An important part of that is that He also sees you as someone to whom He will give anything as long as it is in His will.

> [32] He who didn't spare his own Son, but delivered him up for us all, how would he not also with him freely give us all things?   Romans 8:32 WEB

When you think about how much he values you, please consider who has valued you so very highly. If someone of high esteem values us highly, it seems to carry more weight than if someone of little significance values us highly. God is just that – God. He is all powerful, all knowing, needs no one, but chooses to invite people to follow Jesus Christ the Messiah as Lord and Savior so that they can be part of His family and spend time with Him. He is not mistaken about you. He gave you your value when He created you.

Also consider a contrast. For most people, the heads of governments will not send a driver to you to pick you up and bring you to their private dining room. They are too important and too busy. God is much more important. He is holding the universe together, yet invites you to not only visit, but to come and live with and in Him as part of His family. You are that important to Him. That is how He sees you. That is how personal He is, and how He wants to treat you.

12.1.4 <u>A Peek Into God's Heart for You</u>

The Bible contains many direct passages that directly talk about God's heart for you, and also some snapshots that often get less attention. This passage is in the latter category.

> [16] Then those who feared Yahweh spoke one with another; and Yahweh listened, and heard, and a book of memory was written before him, for those who feared Yahweh, and who honored his name. Malachi 3:16 WEB

The context of the verse is that God is in the middle of describing the judgment He must give to those who have disobeyed Him. His anger is certainly stirred. In the midst of His anger, He hears those who fear Him talking, and His attention is drawn to it.

Now, let's dwell on that a moment. God is not easily distracted, and He does not lose focus. When He does something, no one can turn Him back. He was in the midst of judging, or was just finished. His attention was turned to something, and that something must have been very important to command His attention at that moment.

God never forgets, but He felt that the conversation was so important that a book of remembrance was written about it for the benefit of those who were having the discussion. The way it appears to me in modern terms is that He did the equivalent of journaling the conversation.

Please consider that for a while. He took notes – yes, it was written before Him, but He was supervising the writing to ensure that it was recorded as He wanted it – about a conversation simply because people loved and honored Him. That is how He very likely feels when you or I do the same. Your love for Him is that important to Him, as is mine. That's how much He loves you and me.

I think that the passage shows not only how much He loves, but also the beauty of the way that He loves. In the midst of the display of the power of judgment comes a picture of tenderness that is so poignant that it can bring tears to your eyes if you ponder it. To me it is a revealing peek into God's heart for you and me.

Once you see how God sees you and loves you, you will have a greater desire to hear God and fellowship with Him.

13 HEARING GOD

Hearing God will lead to **being led by the Spirit**. Christians hear God's voice (John 10:27). They can train that hearing by becoming very familiar with God's word. The subject is covered in much greater detail in my book *Discipling Muslim Background Believers*.

MBBs, like all Christians, need to know how to be led by the Holy Spirit and also to grow in that knowledge. This type of growth is a lifelong process.

Being led by the Spirit is not a set of rules – it is relational. It is much like getting to know and understand a good father. You learn who he is and how he generally acts – you learn his ways. In the process you learn how he speaks and what he says. You learn of his love for you, and what being his child means. The main thing that happens as a result is that you enjoy him and want to be with him. You follow him everywhere, and if he asks you to do something you gladly do so because you love him. You are obeying, but it really feels like part of the relationship. You delight to do what he wants because you know that he loves you, is with you, and will do good things for you. You trust him. He is your father.

It is much the same way with God. He sent His Spirit to dwell in us so that He can lead and guide us (John 16:13-16).

There are some things for Christians to do to make it easier to follow that guidance:

1. Get to know the one God – God the Father, Son and Holy Spirit – and His ways better;
2. Get to know His word better;
3. Grow in your ability to **hear His voice**; and
4. Obeying Him in a correct, complete and timely way – all from a place of security in Him.

As mentioned above, learning to be led by the Holy Spirit is a process. It is helped along by an intentional desire to grow spiritually. That comes through a better understanding of God, which can be greatly helped by practicing **spiritual disciplines**. Spiritual disciplines are listed in Chapter 6 above.

14 PRAYER

Prayer is a fundamental part of relating to God. It is essentially asking, and can lead to communication with God when coupled with intimacy with Him and hearing Him, both mentioned in the chapters above.

14.1 WHAT IS PRAYER?

Prayer is part of our intimacy with God. Intimacy implies closeness, but not simply in the sense of nearness. It carries with it the meaning of friendship. As a Christian, we can be friends with God. Jesus said:

> [14] You are my friends, if you do whatever I command you. [15] No longer do I call you servants, for the servant doesn't know what his lord does. But I have called you friends, for everything that I heard from my Father, I have made known to you. John 15:14-15 WEB

Though Jesus is speaking to the disciples, these words also apply to the Christians who came after them, who also do what He commands.

There are many words used for prayer in Hebrew and Greek. They all are translated as "prayer" or "supplication" in

English. Many English dictionaries have broadened the use of these words beyond the original definitions given in Hebrew and Greek lexicons to include all aspects of conversation with God. The actual Greek and Hebrew words all mean, essentially, to ask. That can be seen from the Hebrew and Greek usage of words translated as "prayer".

Below is a list of the main words below with their *Strong's Concordance* numbers:

Hebrew

8605 taphillah = prayer (from 6419 palal = pray or intercede)

6419 palal = pray or intercede

7878 siyach = pray or express contemplated needs

6279 athar = entreat (ask) or supplicate

3908 lachash = prayer (from 3907 lachash (different in Hebrew, but same transliteration) = to whisper)

2470 chalah = to be sick or to beg

Granted, the sense of the word "prayer" is not entirely clear from the Hebrew words, but it is made clearer by words in the *Strong's Concordance* Greek lexicon:

Greek

4335 proseuche = prayer addressed to God, a place for such prayer (from 4336)

4336 prosuechomai = wishes extended towards God

1162 deesis = seeking, asking, entreating

The above are the primary Greek words for "prayer", and all have the sense of a person coming to God and uttering a request for a need or wish.

In law, the English word "prayer" is specifically used for asking something from the court.

Prayer is technically asking, and does not involve **listening to God** or God speaking. The latter two are part of a conversation. Prayer, though, can be part of a conversation with God.

Prayer can be based on need spoken from the heart, **or modeled on prayers in the Bible, on the names of God, or the word of God**.

14.2 TO WHOM DO CHRISTIANS PRAY?

In the passage below, Jesus spoke about prayer during the time after His resurrection but before His second coming (we are still in that time):

²³ "In that day you will ask me no questions. Most
certainly I tell you, whatever you may ask of the Father
in my name, he will give it to you. ²⁴ Until now, you
have asked nothing in my name. Ask, and you will
receive, that your joy may be made full. ²⁵ I have spoken
these things to you in figures of speech. But the time is
coming when I will no more speak to you in figures of
speech, but will tell you plainly about the Father. ²⁶ In
that day you will ask in my name; and I don't say to
you, that I will pray to the Father for you, ²⁷ for the
Father himself loves you, because you have loved me,
and have believed that I came from God. John 16:23-27
WEB

Verses 24-27 make it clear that:

1. Christians pray to the Father;
2. In Jesus' name; and
3. Jesus does not ask on our behalf because the Father
    loves us and will answer us directly.

Thus, Christians pray to the Father in Jesus' name.

14.3 PRAYING IN JESUS' NAME

Christians participate in the **new covenant** with God. Because Jesus takes away our sin through the **cross** and gives us new life through His **resurrection**, we become new creations when we repent and turn to Him for **salvation**. This allows us to receive the benefits of the new covenant. One such benefit is the ability to approach God and make requests and receive the same love and consideration from the Father that Jesus would receive. I still find it almost overwhelming that God loves each one of us as much as He loves Jesus, His only begotten Son and God in the form of man.

When we ask in Jesus name, it is not a small addition to a request. It is appealing to God in the legal standing of Jesus. That means that if you ask according to God's will, your prayer will be granted. Saying, "In Jesus' name." at the end of a prayer does not mean it is in His name. His name reflects His character. Prayer in Jesus' name should reflect His will and character, as well as properly reflecting submission to God.

One way to learn this type of prayer is to read and study prayers in the Bible and to see, if possible, how those prayers were answered. Then, use those prayers as an example of how to pray in those same circumstances. I find the prayers in Psalms to be particularly useful for this type of praying.

14.4 HOW TO PRAY

Prayer involves the physical as well as the spirit and mind.

14.4.1 PHYSICAL POSTURE

I think that posture can be important in expressing the heart. Kneeling before God can be an expression of humility.

In Islam, posture is prescribed for many types of prayers. In Christianity, there is no particular posture for a certain type of prayer. The following is a list of several prayer postures in the Bible, with a verse reference to an example of each:

1. Lying down (Psalms 4:4);
2. Face to the ground (Matthew 26:39);
3. Kneeling (Ephesians 3:14);
4. Sitting (2 Samuel 7:18);
5. Standing (Mark 11:25); and
6. Lifting hands (1 Timothy 2:8).

When the disciples asked Jesus how to pray, He gave them a prayer template– the Lord's prayer – that did not mention posture, but rather indicated the type of content and the requester's spiritual posture. Please note that unlike Islamic tradition, there is no prescribed prayer in the Bible for specific times of the day or for specific circumstances. Though certain Christian denominations do use prescribed prayers, the Bible does not require them. It is useful to study those prescribed prayers as examples. Feel free to use them as long as they are not contradicted by the Bible.

14.4.2 SPIRITUAL POSTURE

While God is everywhere and dwells inside a Christian (John 17:23, 26), prayer involves approaching God to ask Him to grant a need or a wish. It is always advisable to approach the Almighty with a very high degree of respect and the right type of **fear of God**. It is also advisable to approach God with **true humility**.

14.4.3 THE LORD'S PRAYER

Jesus taught His disciples to pray. In Matthew 6:5-15, there are many lessons regarding prayer.

> [5] "When you pray, you shall not be as the hypocrites, for they love to stand and pray in the synagogues and in the corners of the streets, that they may be seen by men.

Most certainly, I tell you, they have received their reward. [6] But you, when you pray, enter into your inner room, and having shut your door, pray to your Father who is in secret, and your Father who sees in secret will reward you openly. [7] In praying, don't use vain repetitions, as the Gentiles do; for they think that they will be heard for their much speaking. [8] Therefore don't be like them, for your Father knows what things you need, before you ask him. [9] Pray like this: 'Our Father in heaven, may your name be kept holy. [10] Let your Kingdom come. Let your will be done, as in heaven, so on earth. [11] Give us today our daily bread. [12] Forgive us our debts, as we also forgive our debtors. [13] Bring us not into temptation, but deliver us from the evil one. For yours is the Kingdom, the power, and the glory forever. Amen.'

[14] "For if you forgive men their trespasses, your heavenly Father will also forgive you. [15] But if you don't forgive men their trespasses, neither will your Father forgive your trespasses. Matthew 6:5-15 WEB

When considering this passage, it is important to understand that Jesus was speaking to Hebrews who understood a particular oral tradition. It was common for Hebrews to memorize passages of the Old Testament. In a temple, the

98

priest would refer to the first line of that passage, and the congregation would understand that he was referring to more than just what he said – he might even be referring to the entire passage. For instance, there are songs recorded in the book of Psalms. Psalm 23 would be referred to by the priest simply by saying, "The Lord is my shepherd." Since the congregation probably had that song memorized, they could understand a reference to the whole of Psalm 23 simply by hearing the first line.

In Matthew 6:9-13 above, the prayer that Jesus asked his disciples to use is a prayer of first lines – a prayer template. While many Christians simply recite the prayer, I believe that the prayer is more useful as an outline that a Christian can follow in his or her daily prayer routines.

The following practical guide is based on the passage above, Matthew 6:5-15:

Verses 5-6:

Pray to be seen and heard by God, not to build a reputation with people.

Verse 7:

Pray simply and without repetition, because God hears you.

Verse 8:

> God knows what you need before you ask.
> (So why pray? Some of the reasons include that it glorifies God to answer our prayers (John 14:13), finding His will so that we can pray it is part of our **intimacy with Him**, and asking and then receiving helps build our **faith** and prepares us to **receive** even more from God, our loving Father.)

Verse 9:

> Recognize God is your Father and that He is good and **cares for you**.
> Recognize He is in heaven, the ruler of the world and that **He is holy**.
> Give God **thanksgiving** and **praise**, including things that are personal to you.

Verse 10:

> Ask that **God's purposes** would happen on
> Earth in the same way that they do in heaven,
> including the establishment of His kingdom and
> revelation of and obedience to His will. Ponder
> this, including asking to do your part. Doing
> these things helps remind you of His purposes
> and also helps you to properly prioritize those
> purposes and align yourself with them.

Verse 11:

> Ask God to provide what He wants to give you
> and others for that day – notice the "us". This
> can include needs that can be provided today and
> also for long-term needs that can be partially
> answered today. This approach has a way of
> reducing worry because you focus on fewer
> needs than everything in your life.

Verse 12:

> **Forgive** those who have sinned against you.
> Then ask for forgiveness for your sin by stating

it, saying that you know it was wrong, telling God that you desire to not do it again, that you want to obey Him in that area.

Verse 13:

This request does not indicate that God is the source of temptation – He is not (James 1:13). This request is asking to be led in the paths of good and also a place in prayer to ask for help against the forces of evil. The literal translation of "deliver us from evil" is "deliver us from the evil one". This is the time for spiritual warfare. Praise God as king, the Almighty, and the one who has all glory and is deserving of that glory. Praise Him because He will always be that way.

Verses 14-15:

Jesus emphasizes that forgiveness comes to us in the same way that we forgive others, meaning that it is extremely important that we forgive others fully and immediately. Note that forgiveness is an act of the will. Even if bad feelings remain, they will eventually line up with your intent, even if you have to continue to forgive that person.

Please note that this prayer template is a good guide but not the only way to pray.

14.4.4 MUST EVERY PRAYER FOLLOW THE TEMPLATE IN THE LORD'S PRAYER?

Not every prayer has to follow the template laid out by the Lord's prayer, though it is a very effective guide for daily prayer. In fact, many of the prayers in the Bible use other formats. There is no requirement to pray specific prayers in specific circumstances in the Bible. For instance, in the Psalms there are many instances where it seems that the psalmist, in distress, utters a simple cry for help that is graciously answered by God (*e.g.* Psalm 18:6). There were occasions in my life in which I was so overwhelmed that "Help, God!" was all I could say. He answered those cries for help.

14.4.5 PRAYERS PRAYED IN AGREEMENT WITH OTHERS

When Christians pray God's will together and in agreement, God is manifest in their midst and grants their prayer. Jesus said:

¹⁹ Again, assuredly I tell you, that if two of you will agree on earth concerning anything that they will ask, it will be done for them by my Father who is in heaven. ²⁰ For where two or three are gathered together in my name, there I am in the middle of them." Matthew 18:19-20 WEB

14.4.6 INTERCESSION

Intercession is praying for someone else. It is appearing before God to ask for someone else's need or wish.

14.5 WHEN TO PRAY

Unlike in Islamic tradition, there is no set time to pray. It is common to pray and read the Bible either in the morning or the evening, and to also pray through the day as needed.

14.5.1 PRAY WITHOUT CEASING

There is a passage of scripture that seems impossible regarding prayer:

^{16} Rejoice always. ^{17} Pray without ceasing. ^{18} In everything give thanks, for this is the will of God in Christ Jesus toward you. 1 Thessalonians 5:16-18 WEB

Verse 17, in Greek, has the meaning of praying with no breaks between prayers. The way to fulfill this verse is to trust that the Holy Spirit will pray for us – otherwise we could not sleep, eat, work or do anything else. The Holy Spirit making up our inability is most likely the case, as stated in Romans:

^{26} In the same way, the Spirit also helps our weaknesses, for we don't know how to pray as we ought. But the Spirit himself makes intercession for us with groanings which can't be uttered. ^{27} He who searches the hearts knows what is on the Spirit's mind, because he makes intercession for the saints according to God. Romans 8:26-27 WEB

One of the gifts of the Spirit is tongues. If you can, please also use this gift as a personal prayer language, asking God to reveal the prayer interpretation to you (the revelation may not always happen at the same time as the prayer).

14.6 SOME BIBLE VERSES TO READ ABOUT PRAYER

Below is a list of verses in the Bible about prayer or containing prayers that can be used as models for prayer for specific things.

Matthew 6:5-14

1 John 1:9

1 John 5:14

Mark 11:22-25

Matthew 18:19-20

Luke 18:9

John 14:13

Philippians 4:6-7

Ephesians 1:15-23

Ephesians 3:14-21

James 5:13-18

Luke 5:16

Ephesians 6:18-20

Luke 11:9-13

Romans 8:26

James 4:3

1 Thessalonians 5:16-18

Discipling Muslim Background Believers contains useful information regarding **what to do when waiting for God to answer your prayers** as well as **what to do when your prayers are not answered the way you had asked**.

15 THE CHURCH IS HIS BODY

In this context, the church is all of the people who follow Jesus Christ the Messiah as Lord and Savior. The **church** is the body of Christ. It is united in the sense that God indwells each Christian. Christians all have different **gifts**. No person has them all, and all the gifts are needed for the body of Christ to function properly. Christians are to **love and serve** not only Christians, but all people. We are to **continue to meet together**, and even **secret believers** need **fellowship**. Much more on church life is in my book *Discipling Muslim Background Believers*, including, among others, **keeping faith pure against syncretism; ministry to the poor, widows, orphans, prisoners**, and the **sick; selecting and appointing leaders; proper use of authority; choosing a good church; and church growth.**

16 FINDING YOUR GIFTS

To effectively serve in the body of Christ, you need to know your spiritual giftings.

The Holy Spirit gives spiritual gifts, some of which are permanent and some of which are for particular situations.

> [5] There are various kinds of service, and the same Lord. [6] There are various kinds of workings, but the same God, who works all things in all. [7] But to each one is given the manifestation of the Spirit for the profit of all. 1 Corinthians 12:5-7 WEB

16.1 PERMANENT GIFTS OF THE HOLY SPIRIT

The permanent gifts are officers and ministry gifts. Ministry gifts are part of the calling of God for an individual. They are powerful but not the same as offices, which are usually given to people for use in significantly growing the church in a large geographic area.

16.1.1 THE GIFTS OF OFFICERS

There are five offices, and a person usually occupies only one at a time. They are to equip the saints, and build up the body of Christ until the church is united in faith and its members are walking in maturity and the fulness of Christ. There are very few of these.

> [11] He gave some to be apostles; and some, prophets; and some, evangelists; and some, shepherds and teachers; [12] for the perfecting of the saints, to the work of serving, to the building up of the body of Christ; [13] until we all attain to the unity of the faith, and of the knowledge of the Son of God, to a full grown man, to the measure of the stature of the fullness of Christ; Ephesians 4:11-13 WEB

Note that He gave "some as". The implication is that the gift, while certainly in the person, is a gift of the person to the church, not the office.

The offices are:

1. Apostles – are involved in starting churches, especially in geographical areas or among people groups where there are none.

2. Prophets – speak on God's behalf and will often bring up appropriate scriptures or convey God's message based on impressions, dreams or visions. They can help churches, groups of people or individuals understand what God has done, is doing and sometimes what God will do.

3. Evangelists – share the good news about salvation and help people become followers of Jesus Christ the Messiah, the Son of the living God. To give you an idea of the level of the gifts in this list, Billy Graham held the office of an evangelist. Though not all offices will have the scope or reach of his ministry, the point is clear – there are not many who hold offices.

4. Pastors – guide Christians into maturity in Christ through taking care of their spiritual and physical needs.

5. Teachers – teach the Bible to Christians so that they can better know and follow God.

16.1.2 THE MINISTRY GIFTS

There are eight ministry gifts. These gifts are for the building up of the church and running it. They are usually associated with a person's calling, and the effects are usually seen frequently in their ministries.

> [27] Now you are the body of Christ, and members individually. [28] God has set some in the assembly: first apostles, second prophets, third teachers, then miracle workers, then gifts of healings, helps, governments, and various kinds of languages. 1 Corinthians 12:27-28 WEB

The ministry gifts are:

1. Apostles – church planters;
2. Prophets – speak God's word;
3. Teachers – teachers of the Bible;
4. Miracles – people gifted in doing supernatural things that usually bring people to salvation;
5. Gifts of healings – people especially gifted in praying for and seeing people get healed;
6. Helps – those who assist others in need;

7. Administrations – those gifted in performing the administrative functions of the church and leading teams; and

8. Various kinds of tongues those gifted in speaking and interpreting tongues.

16.2 THE MANIFESTATIONS OF THE HOLY SPIRIT

The manifestations of the Holy Spirit are gifts He gives for the common good. They are not permanent.

[7] But to each one is given the manifestation of the Spirit for the profit of all. [8] For to one is given through the Spirit the word of wisdom, and to another the word of knowledge, according to the same Spirit; [9] to another faith, by the same Spirit; and to another gifts of healings, by the same Spirit; [10] and to another workings of miracles; and to another prophecy; and to another discerning of spirits; to another different kinds of languages; and to another the interpretation of languages. [11] But the one and the same Spirit produces all of these, distributing to each one separately as he desires. 1 Corinthians 12:7-11 WEB

The manifestations of the Holy Spirit are:

1. word of wisdom – supernaturally knowing how to do something or solve a problem;

2. word of knowledge -- supernaturally knowing something the person did not know;

3. faith – a special gift to believe for something specific, not the same as faith required to know and follow Jesus;

4. gifts of healing – a special ability to pray for various types of physical, mental and emotional hurts;

5. effecting of miracles – the ability to perform special miracles that usually lead people to believe in Jesus Christ the Messiah as Lord and Savior;

6. prophecy – speaking God's word;

7. distinguishing of spirits – being aware of what type of evil spirits are operating in an area or oppressing or possessing a person;

8. various kinds of tongues – the ability to speak known and unknown languages (tongues of angels) that were previously unknown to the speaker (used in a church service – can also be used as a personal prayer language); and

9. interpretation of tongues -- the ability to understand and translate known and unknown languages

(tongues of angels) that were previously unknown to the hearer.

16.3 KNOWING YOUR GIFTS

Knowing your gifts is an exercise in following the Holy Spirit. He will use circumstances and your desires to cause you to pray and do things in Him. As this happens, for instance people getting healed many times when you pray, you can start to think that you might have not just a temporary gift of healing, but also a permanent gift. If you do, pray for guidance about how to use it.

Regarding ministry gifts, there are tests that are available for a fee that can be taken online. One example is S.H.A.P.E., but there are many others.

Once you think you know your ministry and manifestational gifts, seek out **wise, Christian counsel** who know you well, who can confirm whether they think you have the gifts you suspect you might.

16.4 OPERATING IN YOUR GIFTS AND IN YOUR ANOINTING/POSITION

Please read 1 Corinthians 12 -14 (three chapters). The passages suggest that a Christian's motive should always be love, that we should seek spiritual gifts, and use them decently and in an orderly way. The rules of politeness should operate as well. We were all taught not to interrupt, and that holds when two people in a church setting get different but complementary impressions at the same time. One can speak, then the other. If both speak at the same time, nothing will be understood.

The exercise of the manifestational gifts usually takes place among people who believe in their operation. If you are alone, you can grow in your use of them, but it is more difficult. Try to find a fellowship of like-minded believers. There will be mutual encouragement, and also the opportunity to receive any needed fine-tuning or constructive correction in the way that you are using your gifts. Ask God to give you opportunities to serve others with your gifts, and for wisdom, guidance and power while using your gifts. Please also see **baptism of the Holy Spirit**.

There are different levels of using your gifts. They include among others individual, small group, church, people group, nation, and the world. Different people are called to exercise their gifts at different levels. It is not about your value to God, but rather about the type of things you are called to do. It is about function because we are all loved equally – the way He loves Jesus. In the verse below, there is an instruction to prophesy according to the proportion of your faith, indicating different levels.

^{3} For I say, through the grace that was given me, to every man who is among you, not to think of himself more highly than he ought to think; but to think reasonably, as God has apportioned to each person a measure of faith. ^{4} For even as we have many members in one body, and all the members don't have the same function, ^{5} so we, who are many, are one body in Christ, and individually members one of another. ^{6} Having gifts differing according to the grace that was given to us, if prophecy, let us prophesy according to the proportion of our faith; ^{7} or service, let us give ourselves to service; or he who teaches, to his teaching; ^{8} or he who exhorts, to his exhorting: he who gives, let him do it with liberality; he who rules, with diligence; he who shows mercy, with cheerfulness. Romans 12:3-8 WEB

It is best to work up the various levels I listed above with the manifestational gifts. Mature Christians will often confirm your gifting, even asking you to operate at a different level when they notice your gifting and are led by the Lord to do so.

It is important to not try to copy or do another's gift, vision or ministry. Do what you are called to do, and rejoice that you are loved for who you are.

17 SHARING YOUR FAITH AND PRAYER FOR SALVATION

Many Christian efforts to evangelize Muslims end up in fruitless arguments because Christians and Muslims do not have common grounds for understanding God or how to relate to Him. Christians need ways to share the gospel with Muslims without overtly referring to the Bible or the Quran, neither of which is accepted as true by adherents of the other faith. Muslims actively train to deflect overtly Bible-based evangelism methods. There are simple yet effective **evangelism methods** that share common ground without compromising the Bible. These evangelism methods, as well as **my testimony**, are in my book *Discipling Muslim Background Believers*. The methods have been used by me when sharing with Muslims, and the Lord used them to bring the Muslims to salvation in Christ.

One of the easiest methods is to tell your story of salvation and growth in Christ. To tell it, it often works best to tell how things were before following Jesus Christ the Messiah as Lord and Savior, then explain how He led you to Himself, and the changes that you have noticed.

Before sharing the gospel, please consider **praying**, **prayer walking**, **spiritual mapping**, and **spiritual warfare**.

The reason to prepare is so that you have the ability to tell your story well, and within the time that you expect to be sharing. I find it useful to rehearse telling the essentials of Christianity (*see below*) – the gospel, the good news of Christ – in various time frames. If I met a person on a bus, I might want to tell the essentials within thirty seconds, add a few seconds for a very quick version of my story, and be prepared for their response. To do that, I would need to have memorized not only the prayer for salvation, but also the steps that the new Christian should take. It is fairly difficult to go that fast, to sound normal while you are doing it, and to remember everything that you need to say. If you can, record yourself and listen to yourself. Then refine your delivery. Keep cycling through the process until you are satisfied. Please also be ready for a three- to five-minute opportunity to share the gospel, and a full opportunity in which you can take the time to explain and dialogue more with the seeker.

Before praying a prayer for salvation, the person you are sharing with should know and believe the essentials of Christianity.

17.1 ESSENTIAL CHRISTIAN BELIEFS

These are some essential Christian beliefs:

1. There is one God. He is both one essence and three persons at the same time – He is a triune God, at the same time Father, Son and Holy Spirit – the **Trinity**.

2. **God** is good, and He is a rewarder of those who seek him.

> **6** Without faith it is impossible to be well pleasing to him, for he who comes to God must believe that he exists, and that he is a rewarder of those who seek him. Hebrews 11:6 WEB

3. **Jesus** the Messiah has come in the flesh.

4. Jesus was born of a virgin and is therefore both God and man.

5. He died on a cross for all of our **sins**, and our individual **forgiveness** can only come if we ask Jesus Christ the Messiah to be our Lord and Savior.

6. He rose again on the third day to give us new life.

7. If we **repent** of our sins and turn to Jesus Christ the Messiah as our Lord and Savior, we will be **born again**, know God, and be with Him forever.

8. Jesus is the only way to **salvation**, and a Christian cannot follow Jesus and another belief system, person or religion – it is an exclusive relationship. No other religion means that we will follow and

obey Him as our sole source of salvation. We will follow no other way of approaching or knowing God or having eternal life in heaven.

9. Jesus Christ is coming again and will come and get living Christians, **resurrect** dead Christians, give us new bodies, make us His bride, and spend eternity with us.

17.2 PRAYER FOR SALVATION

If a Muslim wants to pray the prayer for salvation, please make sure that you have covered with them **essential Christian beliefs** (*see above*) to ensure that they believe them. Then they can pray the prayer for salvation.

This prayer, or something very similar to it, if prayed with belief and sincerity, will result in the greatest change in the Muslim's life. They will have **salvation**. They will join the family of God, and He will be their **Father** forever.

Someone told me a short while before I prayed a similar prayer that it would be the greatest ride in my life and that I should sit back and enjoy it. That person was right. When the Muslim is ready, please pray with them the prayer below to God – you can simply read it and the Muslim can agree to it.

Gracious God, thank You for your goodness towards me. I believe that You are Father, Son, and Holy Spirit. I believe that You sent Jesus Christ the Messiah, Your Son, to Earth. I believe that He was born of a virgin. I believe that He died on a cross to pay for the sins of the world, including mine. I believe that Jesus Christ the Messiah rose from the grave on the third day to give life to those who believe in Him and follow Him as Lord. I believe that Jesus Christ the Messiah will return. I turn away from all of my sin and ask that You would forgive me. I turn to You. I call Jesus Christ the Messiah my Lord and Savior, and ask that You, Father, Son and Holy Spirit would save me. I want to obey Jesus as God, and follow His teachings and those in the Bible. Thank You, Father, Son, and Holy Spirit, for saving me.

If they sincerely believed the essential Christian beliefs and sincerely prayed the above prayer or something similar to it, then they are now changed. They are **born again**, and are a part of God's family. They are saved, and are a Christian.

They do not have to keep praying this prayer. It is a solemn commitment that only needs to be lived out daily rather than made anew daily.

17.3 STEPS TO TAKE AFTER SALVATION

Here are some steps for the seeker to take after praying a prayer for salvation:

1. Get to know **God** better.

   1.1 Read the **Bible**.

   1.2 Communication and **intimacy with God**.

2. Get **baptized**.

3. Find **fellowship** if you can.

4. Take **communion**.

5. Seek the **baptism of the Holy Spirit**.

6. Follow the steps in the **Reading Path for MBB Discipleship**. It will suggest where and how to start your journey as a Christian.

I have also written a Bible study that complements the above reading path from my book *Discipling Muslim Background Believers*. The book is called *Muslim Background Believer Bible Studies*.

The MBB should try to find a discipleship group or **small group**. This group may need to be secret, meet secretly, and use secret communication methods – circumstances may require that the MBB become a **secret believer** for a while. If so, my book *Discipling Muslim Background Believers* will be very useful because it contains guidance on preparing to be a secret believer, advice on avoiding syncretism, and guidance about living as a fruitful Christian while keeping faith secret from some or many people. It also helps decide when to stop living as a secret believer.

It is important to note that once a Muslim becomes an MBB, there may be a period during which they feel disoriented because the Quran is no longer their guide. The Quran is very specific about some daily tasks, whereas the Bible essentially provides principles. They will need help finding what the Bible says, and quickly. *Discipling Muslim Background Believers* has a helpful index containing concepts and words, and also a glossary. It can be a useful reference as the MBB grows in discipleship.

18 <u>MINISTERING TO OTHERS</u>

Ministering to others is not difficult, nor does it need the same training that a professional pastor receives. It is showing the love of God to people and letting the Holy Spirit move through you. The basics involve seeing a need, being **led by the Holy Spirit** to meet the need, then operating in the **gifts that the Holy Spirit gave you** to meet the need.

Before ministering to others, please consider **praying, prayer walking**, **spiritual mapping**, and **spiritual warfare**.

You can minister to others by **serving** at a church or in a small group, ministering to individuals who need **prayer** or even healing, **evangelizing**, **starting small groups or even churches**.

For all of the above ministry, whether alone, with others, planned or sudden, ask God to **anoint or baptize you with the Holy Spirit**, give you wisdom and guidance, protection, and to open effective doors of ministry (1 Corinthians 16:9) for you so that you can do the good works He wants done by you (Ephesians 2:10).

19 TITHING AND GIVING

Tithing is giving ten percent of your total earnings to the church for the operation of its ministries and administration. Giving is amounts you give above that.

Tithing is a **spiritual discipline**. Tithing and giving should be done from the heart, joyfully and without complaint, because God loves a cheerful giver (2 Corinthians 9:7).

20 SPIRITUAL AUTHORITY

All **authority** comes from God, who delegates it to **leaders** in **families**, **churches**, organizations and governments.

In the context of Christianity, authority is a God-given delegation of responsibility and power to achieve a specific task or ministry. Please note that you do not own the task – God does. You are a steward, one who acts on behalf of and for the benefit of another. This means that if He gives you authority, you must use it appropriately. Appropriate use of authority involves at least the following:

1. Loving and serving those under your authority;

2. Staying within the bounds of your authority – do not think because you have authority in one area that you can exercise authority and oversight in another area;

3. Remembering that the goal is to build up and encourage others, not lord over them (1 Peter 5:3);

4. Being diligent to fully do what God has called you to do and not turning back from the task;

5. Recognizing that you will require the help of others and making sure to give credit where it is due.

Authority can be **abused**, and has terrible consequences when that happens – both for the abused and for the leader when God deals with him or her. The abuser will be brought to repentance or to correction that leads to repentance.

21 MARRIAGE

Marriage was created by God, and Christians consider it a sacred thing. It is designed and directed by God to be between one man and one woman. Christians should only marry Christians (2 Corinthians 6:14 and 1 Corinthians 7:12-14). Genesis 1-2 show the creation of man and woman, and their union. Ephesians chapters 5-6 speak of the marriage relationship, as well as parenting. The relationship of a husband and wife reflect the mystery of Christ and His church. Forced marriage to a non-Christian must be rejected, even if you must flee. If you do need to flee, please read the relevant portions of **persecution**.

It is important to see that just prior to telling wives to submit to husbands, there is an overriding principle:

> [21] subjecting yourselves to one another in the fear of
> Christ. Ephesians 5:21 WEB

This means that husbands and wives submit to each other as the main principle. Men and women are equal in authority in most spheres except in the home, where women submit to the husband's gentle guidance if they disagree about spiritual matters, usually big decisions, when no agreement can be reached after significant discussion in which both sides have had the opportunity to fully express their thoughts.

Though the man, in the home, has authority over the wife and is held accountable for his spiritual decisions, he cannot boss his wife around. He has to love her in the same manner as Christ loved the church. Jesus loved and served the church sacrificially, and so should the husband.

Men are commanded to love their wives, while women are commanded to respect their husbands. In other places, Christians are commanded to love others in the manner they wish to be treated, and that includes respect. Marriage involves mutual love and respect.

There is much more detail on family matters in **family life**.

22 GROWTH TEMPLATE FOR SMALL GROUPS

Christians were created to be in community, the **body of Christ**. Many of our **fellowship** needs can be met in **small groups**. For many MBBs, there will be no church or small group nearby. If there is, they may not want to go there for various reasons. If so, they should conduct **evangelism** in their **affinity group** – their group of relatives and friends – as the **Lord leads** in **wisdom**. The group can start as a **seeker small group**, which may need to use methods described in **secret believer** in order to keep confidential the seeker's inquiry into Christ.

Once the group reaches sixteen to twenty MBBs through outreach, it should multiply, becoming two groups of eight to ten MBBs. This number is small enough to allow all the members of the group to participate, and large enough to have a diverse set of gifts operating in the group.

A template for **multiplying small group Bible studies** can be found in my book *Discipling Muslim Background Believers*. Once there are **enough small groups, a church can be formed** (I recommend about 100-120 groups or around 1,000 people so that the church can withstand persecution).

23 SELECTING LEADERS

Leaders will need to be selected for small groups and churches. Please **pray** over your selections, and consider engaging in **spiritual warfare** before **selecting and appointing leaders for small groups** as well as **selecting and appointing leaders for churches**.

It is especially important to appoint leaders with good character. Having skills is important, but they can be learned. Character is not learned easily.

24 SENDING PEOPLE OUT

When an area experiences **multiplication of small groups** and **church growth**, there is a need to send people out with a blessing and also to follow-up with them. The follow-up process is in the bolded sections of my book *Discipling Muslim Background Believers*. If possible, please consider taking a collection of money to give as a gift to the new group to help it get established more quickly.

25 <u>SOME IMPORTANT</u> <u>CONSIDERATIONS</u>

There will be **problematic issues and considerations** that the discipler will need to know about and review prior to discipling someone. Among the many will be **persecution**, and another will be to understand the needs of someone who needs to be a **secret believer**.

The discipler should also be very familiar with the **list of major Quranic substitutions**, which is an appendix.

Descriptions of my other books are on the end pages of this book.

BOOKS

DISCIPLING
MUSLIM
BACKGROUND
BELIEVERS

Abu Da'ud

This book can be purchased:

- From my website, abudaud.com, in EPUB and
  MOBI (Amazon Kindle format); or
- From Amazon in MOBI (Amazon Kindle format) or
  in paperback.

MUSLIM BACKGROUND BELIEVER BIBLE STUDIES

Abu Da'ud

This book can be purchased:

- From my website, abudaud.com, in EPUB and MOBI (Amazon Kindle format); or
- From Amazon in MOBI (Amazon Kindle format) or in paperback.

MUSLIM SEEKER BIBLE STUDY

Abu Da'ud

This book can be purchased:

- From my website, abudaud.com, in EPUB and MOBI (Amazon Kindle format); or
- From Amazon in MOBI (Amazon Kindle format) or in paperback.

OVERVIEW OF DISCIPLESHIP IN DISCIPLING MUSLIM BACKGROUND BELIEVERS

Abu Da'ud

This book can be purchased:

- From my website, abudaud.com, in EPUB and MOBI (Amazon Kindle format); or
- From Amazon in MOBI (Amazon Kindle format) or in paperback.

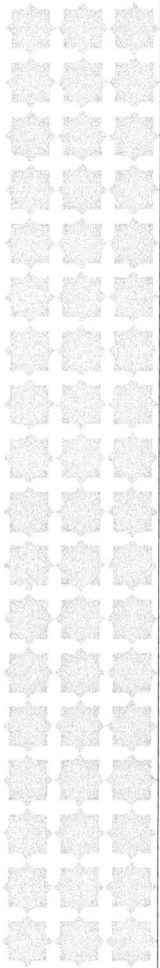

OVERVIEW OF
SEEKER
EVANGELISM
IN
DISCIPLING
MUSLIM
BACKGROUND
BELIEVERS

Abu Da'ud

This book can be purchased:

- From my website, abudaud.com, in EPUB and
  MOBI (Amazon Kindle format); or
- From Amazon in MOBI (Amazon Kindle format) or
  in paperback.

ABOUT THE AUTHOR

Abu Da'ud is a former Muslim, born and raised in a Muslim majority country, with family members from both the Sunni and Shia branches of Islam. He was raised Sunni and was also taught Shia Islam. He is the only Christian known on either side of his family and has been a Christian for nearly forty years. His parents disowned and disinherited him once they discovered he became a Christian.

By God's grace, he did the ministry below and gives Him all the glory:

- Led more than 50 Muslims to the Lord
- Led over 1,000 people to the Lord
- Discipled Muslims and others
- Led
  - weekly refugee ministry for Muslim and MBBs
  - small groups
- Taught
  - Muslim ministry class at a large church (10,000+)
  - Bible study class for Muslim college students
  - Perspectives on the World Christian Movement course

- Started a small church